TOLSTOY

BY L. WINSTANLEY, M.A.

LECTURER IN ENGLISH

THE UNIVERSITY COLLEGE OF WALES, ABERYSTWYTH

MT. SAN ANTONIO COLLEGE

TOLSTOY

Format Copyright © 2021 by MSAC Philosophy Group

First Edition | Trade paperback

ISBN: 978-1-56543-293-2

General Editors: Dr. Andrea Diem and Dr. David Lane

MSAC Philosophy Group was founded in 1990 and is designed to provide a wide range of materials (from books to magazines to films to audio presentations to interactive texts) on such subjects as evolutionary biology, quantum theory, neuroscience, and critical studies in religion and philosophy. All books are sold on a not for profit basis. Free PDF versions are made available whenever possible. In addition, there is a growing collection of audio books specifically created for students at Mt. San Antonio College and the community at large. A large series of original movies have also been produced which touch on such topics as artificial intelligence, eliminative materialism, consciousness, and skepticism.

DEDICATED TO MY BELOVED FRIEND

ANNA BRODSKY

Tolstoy

CONTENTS

I. TOLSTOY'S CONTEMPORARIES

II. LIFE OF TOLSTOY—"A LANDED PROPRIETOR"—"CHILDHOOD"—"THE COSSACKS"—"TALES FROM SEBASTOPOL"

III. LIFE OF TOLSTOY (*continued*)—JOURNEY ABROAD—PEASANT SCHOOLS—"TALES FOR CHILDREN"—MARRIED LIFE—RELIGIOUS DIFFICULTIES—CONVERSION

IV. "WAR AND PEACE"

V. "ANNA KARÉNINA"

VI. "MY CONFESSION"—"MY RELIGION"—"WHAT IS ART?" ETC.

VII. "THE POWER OF DARKNESS"—"THE KREUTZER SONATA"—"RESURRECTION"

VIII. THE INFLUENCE OF TOLSTOY

BIBLIOGRAPHY

CHAPTER I

TOLSTOY'S CONTEMPORARIES

The most striking literary phenomenon of the nineteenth century is, undoubtedly, the rise into power and prominence of Russian authors.

Some fifty years ago Russian literature was practically unknown to Western Europe; by the majority of people its very existence seems to have been unsuspected; we find even so great an adventurer as Carlyle, himself guiding his countrymen to many new tracts of literary discovery, speaking of "the great silent Russians who are drilling a whole continent into obedience, but who have produced 'nothing articulate' as yet." In less than thirty years from the time when Carlyle penned that sentence Russian literature had become recognised as one of the most powerful and vital in Europe; its influence, already enormous, increases every day; it is great in France, in Germany, in Scandinavia, even in conservative England; hardly since the Renaissance has Europe beheld such a phenomenon—a literary advance at once so rapid and so great.

The truth is that we have seen in Russia a growth very similar to that which occurred in Western Europe at the time of the Renaissance. In the fifteenth and sixteenth centuries Europe as a whole experienced the vivifying influence of two great literatures—Greek and Latin—and it had, at the same time, a mode of life to depict and ideas of life to express which differed widely from those of the classical nations: the great models showed them the fascination of poetry and art, and stimulated them to production; the different conditions of life, the varying ideals, prevented their production from becoming a mere imitation, and made it new, significant, and vital. Something very similar has occurred hi modern Russia. Russia has had the stimulus of Western Europe—especially of

England and France—but, at the same time, the conditions of its life are so powerfully individual, so exceedingly unlike those of England and France, that its authors are hardly even tempted to produce work which is a mere imitation; as soon as they observe at all, the result of their observations is bound to be different. Their production is thus distinctive and individual, and, in its own turn, reacts upon the literatures which first inspired it.

The chief literary form in the later nineteenth century has been the psychological novel, and it is this which the Russians have taken up, developed, and almost recreated.

In psychology Russian writers are greatly helped by their own exceeding truthfulness and candour. France and England are lands of complex civilisations, of many social grades and many conventions, and the mental attitude of their writers is, almost inevitably, conventional, and thus, to a certain extent, insincere. Russian life has far fewer social grades and far fewer conventions; Russian writers are, beyond comparison, more candid with themselves and with others; they speak the exact truth with a *naïveté* almost resembling the *naïveté* of children, but with the far-reaching intelligence of maturity. This invaluable quality of sincerity is found in all the greatest Russians; Tolstoy and Dostoïevsky, in especial, hide nothing, but reproduce all they know with an absence of self-consciousness that amazes even while it fascinates.

We all of us know in our hearts that this profound sincerity is essential to really great literature; but, none the less, we, in a variety of ways, discourage and forbid it: in prudish England an author is always afraid of offending "moral" prejudices; in France writers, though in moral respects far freer, are most sensitively afraid of appearing ridiculous or absurd. To a Russian neither of these fears would seem to exist. Throughout his work Tolstoy insists with the most vehement intensity that absolute truthfulness in all respects is the essential foundation of morals, and nothing angers him more than concealment, which he declares to be, always and everywhere, the assistant and protector of vice, while the fear of being absurd he dismisses as one of the most ridiculous vanities of adolescence, unworthy of a sane man.

Another quality that greatly assists Russian writers is their unique gift of sympathy; there may be, probably there is, something in the very fibre of the race essentially feminine and sensitive, but the peculiar conditions of their government account for much. Russia is the nation which, above all other great nations in our days, has the most tragic destiny, suffers most deeply and undeservedly; it is probably this which helps to give her great writers so deep a compassion; they penetrate to the very foundation of human experience, they fathom the deepest abysses of human suffering, and they return with an unequalled tenderness, with a noble beauty of compassion, which has, in the modern world, no rival at all.

It is worthy of note that the ancient Greeks would appear to have gained in a similar way some of the greatest qualities in their national soul. They too had the experience of a deep suffering; they stood between East and West, they bore the brunt of long-lasting racial conflicts, and, when they finally emerged triumphant, they carried with them the beautiful fruit of that bitter experience, in their profound understanding of human suffering, and their knowledge of all the depths of tragedy. They too gain from their own anguish a unique tenderness and compassion; Priam kissing the hands of Achilles, "terrible man-slaying that had slain so many of his sons," is one of the world's supreme types of pathos; this lovely tenderness illumines all the great Greek poetry from Homer to Euripides.

Latin literature, in comparison with the Greek, is wanting both in compassion and in depth, but the Romans had never in the same way suffered, and they knew less of the secrets of the human soul.

Tolstoy, we are told, read much in Homer, and was greatly influenced by him in writing his *War and Peace*. It is hardly surprising, for, notwithstanding all differences, there is a considerable similarity—the two are alike in their heroism, in their understanding of war, their vast and crowded canvas, their tragic view of human destiny, and their lovely compassion. It is characteristic of the Russian breadth of mind and elemental sincerity that Tolstoy really can take Homer as his model in writing a modern novel. It is hardly necessary to remark that he has not Homer's sense of beauty, but who in this modern world has?

The fecundity of Russian literature is very great; it is a great mistake to regard Tolstoy as if he stood alone; like Shakespeare, Tolstoy is only the highest peak, or perhaps we should say the greatest magnitude, among a number of writers only less distinguished than himself.

Among Tolstoy's predecessors the Russians themselves rank Gogol very high; he owes much to the influence of Dickens; his books show endless comic verve, are crowded with situations full of laughter, but at the same time he has, in general, a very serious purpose behind. Gogol, though humane and good-tempered, is a keen satirist; comparatively little known abroad, he is greatly loved by Russians themselves.

Among Tolstoy's leading contemporaries the man whom, above all others, he most whole-heartedly admired was Féodor Dostoïevsky. Dostoïevsky had a tragic history which is reflected in his works; he was involved in the plots of the Decembrists, condemned to execution, and only at the last moment reprieved; for the remainder of his life, possibly in consequence of the shock to his nervous system, he became an epileptic; he was exiled for a time to Siberia.

Dostoïevsky's books are largely studies in crime, but quite unlike those familiar to our modern press; the modern detective story with its police-court atmosphere and its vulgar shallowness of interest belongs to a world immeasurably beneath Dostoïevsky; even the world of tragic crime, depicted so forcibly by the Elizabethans, stands far apart from his; in Elizabethan dramas crime is observed for the sake of its passion, it is invested with a terrible though gloomy allurement, and its end is the ruin of the noblest or the tragic destruction of a human soul.

Dostoïevsky's novels of crime are really studies in redemption: in *Crime and Punishment* the hero is a murderer and the heroine a fallen woman, but both ultimately work out their salvation. To Dostoïevsky crime is a moral disease, a source of the most exquisite suffering to the soul; he studies the process by which the soul, sick to death and horribly distressed, purifies and cleanses itself. Dostoïevsky is not, like the Elizabethans, impressed by the tragic beauty of crime; on the contrary, he realises and makes us realise its loathsomeness, its sordid horror; but, notwithstanding its dark and gloomy setting, his work is in essence far from pessimistic; the expiatory power of suffering, the innate nobility of the human soul, the miserable meanness of sin, the beauty of compassion—these are the impressions which he prints most deeply in the mind.

The nearest western parallel is to be found, no doubt, in Victor Hugo's *Les Misérables*, where the redemption of a human soul is, in somewhat similar method, described; but Victor Hugo does not penetrate to the foundations of human life in the same manner as Dostoïevsky; he—the petted idol of the French public—had not that first-hand acquaintance with the terrible realities of oppression; there is something theatrical and rhetorical, almost insincere, about Hugo if we compare him with the great Russian.

It is worthy of observation that Tolstoy greatly admired both *Les Misérables* and Dostoïevsky; the older he grew and the more powerfully the influence of the latter became manifest, his sympathy with the oppressed, his interest in redemption, increased, until in the last of his great novels, *Resurrection*, we find that he writes in the very spirit of Dostoïevsky; his heroine goes down to the depths of shame and degradation, and yet is redeemed and restored. The pessimist may perhaps declare that both Tolstoy and Dostoïevsky are mistaken in thinking that a human being can sink so low and yet be redeemed; to which it can only be replied that the unflinching courage with which they face realities—all realities, however horrible and sordid—earns them their right to be believed when they assert the restorative power of purity and love.

Amid all Tolstoy's contemporaries the one most widely appreciated in Europe is, without doubt, Turgénief. He was understood earlier and more readily than his fellow-countrymen, this appreciation being no doubt due to the fact that there is more foreign influence in his work, and that he is less purely Russian. Turgénief owes much to French literature; the influence of its clarity of style, its artistic form, its sense of proportion, are evident throughout his writing; he is the most artistic and literary of Russian authors, but, strong as the French influence is in his work, no one could ever mistake him for a Frenchman; he has the depth and tenderness of the Slavonic temperament, its moral earnestness, its profound sincerity.

Turgénief and Tolstoy were exceedingly unlike in life and work; it is not surprising that, when they met, they were alternately fascinated and repelled. Turgénief complained that Tolstoy pursued him like a woman in love and yet, when they were together, was always quarrelling with him. At one time they were devoted friends, at another they came near to fighting a duel. Russia might well have been horrified by the spectacle of her two greatest men of genius destroying each other; their friends intervened and separated them, but the reconciliation was never quite complete. The same opposition of personality can be plainly perceived in their work. Tolstoy is by far the more masculine genius, enormous in his vitality and power, immense in his canvases; he loves, in his early work especially, to study masculine and virile characters, to dwell on war and hunting, and all the vigorous activities of men; his heroines, charming as they often are, are rarely or never heroic; they are nearly always dominated by their own emotions, they yield only too thoroughly to the men who, with a cruel masculine egoism, at once love and destroy them. Again it is hardly until he reaches *Resurrection* that he shows a true sense of the value of women as individuals: in his earlier novels he consents to value them only in their maternal aspect, as the mothers of men. His conception of love is nearly always a masculine passion with, it must be acknowledged, a somewhat crude masculinity; it is a disturbance of the senses rather than an emotion of the soul (Plato would have classed it unquestioningly as born of the lower Aphrodite), and Tolstoy's finest heroes nearly always yield to it reluctantly and, as it were, churlishly.

Like another great masculine genius—Milton—Tolstoy feels most intimately, but shudders at the power that women possess over men. How often in his works one meets with women who are like Milton's Dalila, possessed of a charm that is mixed with loathing and disgust. Both Milton and Tolstoy regard with horror, as one of the worst of snares, the idealising power of love.

Turgénief is very different. He has not Tolstoy's enormous vitality nor his immense scope; his novels are, in comparison, quite brief, and some of his best work is done in a very small compass, though it is always so deep in meaning that it never seems slight. He has achieved nothing more perfect than the little story of *Faust*, which might, so far as length goes, be only a French *feuilleton*. He is always and essentially poetic; one of the keenest of all human observers, he dislikes sordid realism; he avoids war and all other forms of extreme violence; it is quite characteristic of him that when he does, for once, choose a soldier hero—Insarov in *On the Eve*—he does not accompany him to war, but makes him die of consumption before the conflict actually begins. Love plays a far larger part in his work than in that of Tolstoy, and it is an altogether nobler kind of love. As a lover, indeed, he belongs to the great poetic idealists, he is of the same race as Dante, as Shakespeare, as Shelley. He understands, quite as well as Tolstoy, the dreadful glamour of an evil passion; he understands how it leads to atrophy of the heart, to desolation and to ruin; but he understands also that nobler passion whose very existence Tolstoy explicitly and vehemently denies—the love which belongs both to the senses and to the soul. Passion in Tolstoy is always a concession to the animal in man; in Turgénief it is often his redemption. It follows from this that he understands women far better than Tolstoy; indeed Turgénief lays his main stress on feminine rather than on masculine character, and the most heroic and beautiful figures in his pages are usually those of women. He draws them, indeed, with a Shakespearean strength and delicacy; he does not regret the influence they have over man's life—it is so often for good; even when he draws the destructive siren who lures men to their doom, he draws her without the Tolstoyan frenzy of hate; he gives her the same kind of charm that Shakespeare gave Cleopatra, and permits her poetry to fascinate even while he shows with the clearest irony all her sensuality and her falseness. It is worthy of note that neither Tolstoy nor Turgénief wholly escape from the influence of their rank. Widely democratic as they are in sympathies they yet betray their aristocratic birth—Tolstoy in the wrath and anger, the almost Satanic fury he turns upon those with whom he happens to disagree, and Turgénief in the fastidious delicacy with which he loves the beautiful, the distinguished, and the rare.

It is Dostoïevsky who is truly the man of the people; he sees through all the cheats of power, but he hates no one; he loves purity and beauty, but he finds them even in the foulest prisons and the lowest slums; of the three he is the truest democrat.

CHAPTER II

LIFE OF TOLSTOY—"A LANDED PROPRIETOR"—"CHILDHOOD"—"THE COSSACKS"—"TALES FROM SEBASTOPOL"

Leo Tolstoy was born August 28, 1828, at the village of Yasnaya Polyana, not far from Tula, on the old main road to Kieff.

His parents were Count Nicolas Tolstoy and Princess Marie Volkonsky, both of them members of well-known families. The Tolstoy family had played a famous, though at times a questionable part in Russian history; its first Count—Peter Tolstoy—was an accomplice in the assassination of the Tsarevitch Alexis, son of Peter the Great; he was appointed Chief of the Secret Service, and, later on, enjoyed the confidence of the Empress Catherine I. When Peter II, son of the murdered Alexis, ascended the throne, Count Tolstoy lost his great position; being at that time an old man, he retired to the monastery of Solovetsky on the White Sea, where he died. The Tolstoy family were, for a period, deprived of their title, but it was restored in the reign of the Empress Elizabeth, daughter of Peter the Great.

The Princess Marie Volkonsky also came of an eminent family; they traced their descent from Rurik, and several of her near relatives had been great generals.

The novelist's father, Nicolas Tolstoy, served in the great campaigns of 1813 and 1814; he was taken prisoner by the French but liberated in 1815, when the allied armies entered Paris. Tolstoy has depicted a number of his relatives in the novel of *War and Peace*; his father is Nicolas Rostof and his mother the Princess Mariya Bolkonsky; in real life as in the book, this mother appears to have been the more remarkable of the two parents, a woman possessed of a singularly noble and beautiful character. Leo was only eighteen months old at the time of his mother's death, but, from what his aunts and other relatives told him, he created a portrait which, whether accurate or not, is of unforgettable charm.

The father died when Leo had reached the age of nine, and the children—four brothers and a sister—were left to the guardianship of their father's sister; they were, as a matter of fact, brought up mainly by a lady named Tatiana Yergolsky, whom they called "aunt," but who was, in reality, only a distant relative. Tatiana Yergolsky had a romantic history; she loved Count Nicolas Tolstoy, and he returned her affection, but she sacrificed herself in order that he might marry the wealthy heiress, Princess Marie Volkonsky. After the marriage she remained an inmate of her cousin's house and won the deep affection of his wife; when a widower Count Nicolas once more desired to marry Tatiana, but she still refused, fearing to spoil the tenderness of her relation to the dead wife and to the children. It would be difficult to imagine a character more sweet and self-sacrificing; upon the orphaned children she bestowed a devoted love; to Leo she took the place of the mother he had never known, and the father he had lost so soon; she was the chief happiness of his childhood, and he declares that, in the building up of his moral character, she, of all human beings, played the most beneficent part.

He says: "Aunt Tatiana had the greatest influence on my life. It was she who taught me while yet in my childhood the moral joy of love. Not by words but by her whole being she imbued me with love. I saw, I felt how happy she was in loving, and I understood the joy of love. That was the first lesson. And the second was that she taught me the beauty of a quiet, lonely life."

The four Tolstoy brothers possessed strong individualities, and Tolstoy had a keen feeling of affection for all the members of his family; his favourite brother was, however, Nicolas—some six years older than himself. He and Nicolas, in their child's play, founded a society which they called "Ant-Brothers," which was to embrace all mankind and all the earth in a loving union; they buried a green stick as a kind of charm to celebrate the founding of this society. When Tolstoy came to die he asked that he might be buried on the hill where, so long ago, he and Nicolas had placed the green stick; it will, at any rate, be one of the world's great places of pilgrimage.

Nicolas possessed great talents; Leo always generously and obstinately believed this brother more gifted than himself, and quotes, with warm approval, Turgénief's opinion: "Turgénief quite correctly observed that he only lacked the imperfections necessary for the making of an author. He did not possess the principal and necessary defect—vanity. But the qualities of an author which he did possess were a refined artistic instinct, an exceedingly delicate sense of proportion, a good-natured gay humour, exceptional and inexhaustible imagination and high moral conceptions, and all this without any conceit. He had such an imagination that for hours he could tell humorous tales and ghost stories."

Tatiana Yergolsky was exceedingly religious, and one of the customs of Yasnaya Polyana was to extend hospitality to all types of pilgrims—monks and nuns and beggars, who led a life of humility and deliberately courted contumely.

Tolstoy's early life was spent in a peculiar poetic and religious atmosphere, an atmosphere mediæval in its tone. This should never be forgotten, for, after a whole lifetime of experience and achievement, we find him returning once more to the beliefs of his youth, stripping them of supernaturalism and ecclesiasticism, but holding with all his heart to the virtues of these pilgrim friends—humility and simplicity and love.

The Tolstoy brothers all went in turn to the university of Kazan. Leo first chose the faculty of Eastern languages, intending to enter the diplomatic service; he then tried law and other courses, but was capricious and unsuccessful; few great writers have ever cared so little for studies or been so scornful of intellectual attainment in others. Tolstoy left the university in disgust, and returned for a time to Yasnaya Polyana, intending to devote himself to his peasants.

There is a study of his life at this period in the book entitled *A Landed Proprietor*, which gives an account, at once graphic and sombre, of the enormous difficulties of the task. We are shown typical days in the life of the hero— Nekhlúdof—as he visits the peasants who have asked for his aid. Many of them live in wretched hovels—this, for example, is the house of one Churis: "The uneven, smoke-begrimed walls of the dwelling were hung with various rags and clothes; in the living-room the walls were literally covered with reddish cockroaches, clustering around the holy images and benches.... In the middle of this dark foetid apartment, not fourteen feet square, was a huge crack in the ceiling; and in spite of the fact that it was braced up in two places, the ceiling hung down so that it threatened to fall from moment to moment.

"'It will crush us to death, it will crush the children,' cried the woman."

Nekhlúdof is annoyed that Churis should have allowed his house to sink into such a condition, but he discovers that Churis has been ruined through the exactions of a land-agent (employed by Nekhlúdof's grandfather), who had cheated the peasant family out of their best land. We see how early and how decidedly Tolstoy has traced the miseries of the peasants to their landlords' exactions. Yet he does not disguise the faults of the peasants themselves: in another hut which Nekhlúdof visits the owner is thoroughly idle, lying on the oven all day and sleeping; his wife has been worked to death, and the old mother bears all the burden of the house and fields. She begs Nekhlúdof to find her a new daughter-in-law, but, with disgust and anger, he declines to force a fresh martyr into the wretched hovel. The overseer recommends that this particular peasant should be flogged, but the "barin" decides to take him into his own house and try to teach him how to labour. Tolstoy has often been accused of idealising Russian peasants, but, as these most graphic pictures attest, he perceived the worst that could be said. Indeed Turgénief complained of this particular book that it was pessimistic and did not do justice to the peasants.

After a brief space Tolstoy left the country and returned to St. Petersburg, where he plunged into dissipation; it was, morally considered, the most ignominious portion of his life. He confesses in his diary: "I am living like a beast, though not entirely depraved; my studies are nearly all abandoned, and spiritually I am very low."

In his religious work, *My Confession*, he speaks with bitter anger of this period of his life.

"I honestly desired," he says, "to make myself a good and virtuous man; but I was young, I had passions, and I stood alone, altogether alone, in my search after virtue. Every time I tried to express the longings of my heart for a truly virtuous life I was met with contempt and derisive laughter; but directly I gave way to the lowest of my passions I was praised and encouraged.... I cannot now recall those years without a painful feeling of horror and loathing. I put men to death in war, I fought duels to slay others, I lost at cards, wasted my substance wrung from the sweat of peasants, punished the latter cruelly, rioted with loose women, and deceived men. Lying, robbery, adultery of all kinds, drunkenness, violence, and murder, all committed by me, not one crime omitted, and yet I was not the less considered by my equals a comparatively moral man."

We should remember that it is the ascetic Tolstoy who is speaking here and judging his former life with all possible sternness, but there can be little doubt that it was this period which gave him his life-long scorn for the corrupt aristocracy whose whole existence was "a mania of selfishness." Never again did he sink so low.

In the meantime Nicolas Tolstoy was serving with the Russian artillery in the Caucasus; in 1851 he returned home on leave, perceived the danger of the immoral life his brother was leading, and persuaded Leo to join him.

Tolstoy spent nearly three years in the Caucasus, and the fresh, beautiful and poetic life restored him to mental and physical health, and awoke in him both religious and creative power. His first novel, *Childhood*, appeared in 1852, and was at once recognised by leading Russian writers as a work of rare promise and charm. It is largely autobiographical, not in the actual incidents, but in the general circumstances, and especially in the mental development. It is most remarkable for the amazing psychological fidelity with which the impressions of childhood are remembered and recorded; the strong affections for parents and brothers, for sister and teacher, the awe-struck reverence for the crazy pilgrim, Grisha, the first faint gleam of romantic love, the poetry of forest rides, the love of animals, the shuddering physical horror in the face of death, the strange confusion and sadness of loss. Everything is at once realistic and full of romance; Tolstoy has brought before us all the clear-cut sharpness of these early impressions of the world before custom has laid upon them a hand "heavy as frost and deep almost as life."

Tolstoy's life in the Caucasus, in its actual details, provided him with the subject-matter for two of his most fascinating works, *The Cossacks*, and *The Invaders*. These are not among his greatest productions; psychologically and dramatically they cannot equal the later novels, but they stand almost alone in their fresh, pure poetry. In these the remorseless realist shows himself as a romantic adventurer—almost, except for the deeper mentality, a Russian Stevenson; the breath of the mountain and forest, the clear, cold sweetness of dawn blows through their pages; they charm with the sense of great spaces, of gay, glad daring; they are filled, above all, with the intoxication of freedom.

It is one of the secrets of Tolstoy's greatness that he experienced, directly and at first hand, so many different kinds of life, and no change could well have been greater than that from the artificial, feverish, corrupt St. Petersburg to the primitive life of the hunter and mountaineer. The hero, Olyénin, is a reflection of Tolstoy himself. We are told how he delights in the first signs of danger, such as the carrying of weapons, &c. Before he has seen them he cannot believe in the beauty of snow-clad mountains; he thinks it as much a figment of the imagination as the melody of Bach's music or the romantic love of woman, in neither of which he is able to believe. But when he sees the mountains they surpass all he has heard and transcend his wildest dreams; they give him an almost Wordsworthian depth of inspiration. "At first the mountains aroused in Olyénin's mind only a sentiment of wonder, then of delight; but afterwards, as he gazed at this chain of snowy mountains, not piled one upon another, but growing and rising straight out of the steppe, little by little he began to get into the spirit of their beauty and he felt the mountains.... From that moment all that he had seen, all that he had thought, all that he had felt, assumed for him the new, sternly majestic character of the mountains.... 'Now life begins,' seemed to be sounded in his ears by some solemn voice."

He shares in the romantic, adventurous life of the Cossacks, a little tribe barricaded away in their own corner of the world and surrounded by their enemies—the semi-civilised Mohammedans.

The most interesting character in the book is the old Cossack hunter, Yeroshka; whole past ages of the world seem to live again in this primitive and fascinating figure; he takes us back to the very childhood of man. He is so strong that, when he has killed a wild boar weighing three hundred and sixty pounds, he can carry it home on his back. He says to Olyénin: "I will find and show you every sort of animal, every kind of bird, and how and where.... I know it all. I have dogs and two fowling-pieces, and nets, and decoys, and a falcon. I can find the track of any wild beast.... I know where he comes to his lair and where he comes to drink or wallow."

Yeroshka has studied all the wisdom of the animals, he is continually pitting his wits against theirs, and he thinks them, on the whole, much cleverer than men: notwithstanding his hunting he loves all creatures so much that he will save even moths from the flame.

Life in the forest is marvellously described—the misty mornings, the search for the stag's lair, the interpreting of his tracks, the swaying of innumerable boughs, the fear of the wild tribes; it is all here—the forest loneliness, the forest enchantment, the forest terror. Even the tiny gnats which cover Olyénin so that they make him grey from head to foot, have their own peculiar attraction; he grows to feel their stings a part of the forest fascination and freedom; they prevent him from growing somnolent, and keep him alive to that immense joy which he finds everywhere in nature and would not miss even for a moment.

Throughout Tolstoy's later work he hates civilisation, and we understand why; he is always longing to escape from it to the life that is inspired by the immense joy of nature and freshened by hard physical toil. Characteristically enough, Tolstoy will not idealise even what he loves, and he confesses that the mere touch of civilisation spoils his Yeroshka; he cannot live like a modern man, and his hut is filthy.

"On the table were flung his blood-stained coat, a half of a milk cake, and next to it a plucked and torn jackdaw.... On the dirty floor were thrown a net and a few dead pheasants, and a hen wandered about pecking, with its leg fastened to a table leg."

In the forests which he so loves Yeroshka is like a wood-god—strong, wise, and happy—but he has only to touch the ordinary life of man and he becomes a Silenus, debased and drunken.

In 1853 Tolstoy left the Caucasus for the Crimea, the influence of his relatives procuring him a post on the staff of the Commander-in-Chief, Prince Gorchakoff. He could not rest until he reached Sebastopol itself, and he entered it in November 1854. He was often in great danger, for he volunteered for duty on the most dangerous posts, even on the famous fourth bastion, whose horrors have never been surpassed in war.

Tolstoy published his *Tales from Sebastopol* in 1854; this book aroused the attention of the Czar, and gained for the author a considerable literary reputation. But Tolstoy achieved something more than reputation, for his whole nature was deepened and widened; it was Sebastopol which first showed him the heroism and tragedy of human destiny, and taught him his immense appreciation of the common man. For him mere cynicism was henceforth at an end; no man who had beheld the sublime heroism of Sebastopol—twenty-two thousand perishing under fire, as many more suffering hideous tortures on the operating tables (without chloroform) and in the hospitals, all this borne not merely with fortitude, but with cheerfulness, not for the sake of any personal gain, but for the sake of an ideal—the ideal of patriotism—no man who had beheld this could relapse into that cheap cynicism which proclaims the essential worthlessness of the human kind.

Tolstoy begins his studies (and this is quite characteristic of his grim realism) in the hospital, and dwells on the passive endurance which is shown there. He passes on to the emotions of men under fire, and gives a masterly exposition of the psychology of war; the physical shrinking, the consciousness of everything sordid and wretched, the curious elation that follows upon fear, the reckless hilarity and carelessness that mark the new recruit, the seasoned calm of the veteran who is grateful for every day left him of his life, the curious superstitions, not based on any soldier's folklore, but springing up of themselves in an environment where all things are so insecure, the swift and noble friendships broken by the heartrending tragedy of death and, through it all, the sombre pride that men feel in their own superhuman endurance.

Tolstoy describes the actual moment of death in battle with such imaginative vividness that it seems almost impossible a man could so realise it without a personal experience.

We may trace from Sebastopol also Tolstoy's characteristic attitude to war, which is peculiar because it unites such a great appreciation of war as a school of heroic virtue with such a whole-hearted condemnation. Most men are blind either to one side or to the other, but, from the very beginning, Tolstoy keeps both steadily in view. We could not explain the fascination war has possessed for so many of the noblest human minds if it were not for the fact that it is often a school of heroic virtue. Homer himself could hardly better the sublime courage of these Tolstoyan heroes, but Tolstoy's very appreciation teaches him also the vast futility of war; it is such a waste of noble human beings, and the ends for which it is waged are, compared with the tremendous sacrifices it evokes, so childish and futile.

CHAPTER III

LIFE OF TOLSTOY (*continued*)—JOURNEY ABROAD—PEASANT SCHOOLS—"TALES FOR CHILDREN"—MARRIED LIFE—RELIGIOUS DIFFICULTIES—CONVERSION

Soon after the capitulation of Sebastopol, Tolstoy, disgusted, with the mere idea of military glory, left military service and returned to St. Petersburg. He was received into the chief literary society of the day, introduced to Turgénief and the poet Fet, who became his most intimate friend. Tolstoy, however, never cared much for literary society; he spoke of it afterwards very slightingly and even scornfully, and he soon left.

In January 1857 he started on a tour in Europe; he visited Paris, and, while there, witnessed an execution which gave him his life-long horror of capital punishment. He declares that he had previously accepted it as a necessity, but, when he saw the ghastly preparations, when he heard the dull sound made by the head falling into the basket, he realised suddenly that, no matter what laws or customs countenanced this act, it was wrong and would always remain wrong. Even the horrors of war did not inspire him with an aversion quite so sickening; what he so disliked was the cold-blooded, premeditated violence wreaked upon a bound and helpless man.

Tolstoy also visited Switzerland—Geneva and Lucerne. At the latter place he was disagreeably impressed by the arrogance of the English tourists. One of the most charming of his minor tales—a little sketch entitled *Albert*—tells the story of a wandering musician treated with haughty severity by the English and, as the candid narrator admits, entertained by Tolstoy himself, with a somewhat exaggerated and theatrical kindness. It shows Tolstoy's habit of digging down to the very foundations of social life in seeking a remedy for the simplest injustice.

In 1860 consumption declared itself in Nicolas Tolstoy and he was soon seriously ill; he went in search of health to Soden and afterwards to Hyères.

Leo went to help in nursing him, and, on September 20th, Nicolas died in his brother's arms.

This event made a deep and tragic impression upon Tolstoy: it was not only the personal loss, though he loved Nicolas more than any other human being, but the worst horror lay in his brother's fear of death, and in the unavailing struggle against it. The circumstances are described in the death of Nicolas Levin in *Anna Karénina*.

Tolstoy next studied elementary education in France, Germany, and England.

In February 1861 the Russian serfs were liberated, and a new era in Russian history began; Tolstoy tried to play his part by starting peasants' schools upon his estate. In his theories of education he was largely influenced by Rousseau; it was from Rousseau that he obtained his ideas of "freedom," and of permitting unchecked development to the child; he organised his schools in a very original manner, and his theories seem to have had a far-reaching effect on Russian education in making it more free and flexible than that of Western Europe.

The tales he wrote for his peasant children, and embodied in various school-readers, form a charming portion of his work; they are exquisitely simple, and full of that fresh observation of the ways of animals and plants and the ways of children themselves which the young so love.

Among the best are stories of his dogs, Milton and Bulka; tales of bear-hunting and its perils; there is an unforgettable study of the hare and its timid ways, another which tells how mother-wolves train their young to hunt. Nor does Tolstoy limit his sympathies to animals—he can make the trees live for us in the same vivid and forcible way; thus he tells how hundreds of young poplars sprang up around an old poplar which was decaying, and how he ordered the young trees to be cut down since he could see that they were taking the sap from the old one. The young trees resisted stoutly: "Sometimes four of us would try to pull up the roots of some young poplar that had been cut down, and found it impossible; it would resist with all its might and would not die." However he persists in destroying them; the old tree itself dies and Tolstoy comments: "He had been long dying, and was conscious of it, and was giving all his life to his shoots. That was the reason why they had grown so rapidly, and I, who had wished to help him, had only killed all his children."

Perfectly charming also are the little studies of peasant children, such as the boy "Filipok," who is passionately eager to go to school but, when he gets there, cannot say a word through shyness; however they leave him alone, and he comes to himself and makes one of the best scholars.

Tolstoy's own educational experiments were not permitted to continue for long; the officials became jealous of his schools, and they were accordingly closed.

In dividing out the land between the nobles and the peasants many disputes occurred, and Tolstoy offered his services as arbitrator; he incurred a good deal of odium among his aristocratic neighbours because he so often took the part of the poor; he saw how the peasants were steadily cheated out of their fair share of land. It is this unfair division which explains the terrible severity of the Russian famines; the peasant has never been allowed sufficient land to support himself, and he cannot, with his best efforts, keep any reserve for bad times. Tolstoy perceived this and, to the best of his ability, struggled against it; like the heroism of the common soldier at Sebastopol, it served its purpose in making him the ardent champion of the poor.

In the year 1862 Tolstoy married Sophia Behrs, with whose family he had been for some time acquainted; he was thirty-four and his bride eighteen.

There ensued a period of great family happiness and of powerful creative work. It was, in the ordinary sense, the happiest time of Tolstoy's life, though he himself, with his ever-progressing moral development and his ever-increasing idealism, later on condemned its happiness as selfish and enervating.

Tolstoy managed his own estate and, by the testimony of many observers, was exceedingly successful with his stock, his buildings, and his crops; he succeeded also in making his peasants happy and contented. His family was large, and his wife proved herself an admirable mother, devoting herself passionately to her children.

It was during this period that Tolstoy achieved his European reputation as a novelist by producing his two great works of *War and Peace*, 1864-9, and *Anna Karénina*, 1873-6.

Tolstoy was a most conscientious and exacting literary artist. Before writing *War and Peace*, he made careful historical studies; it is his longest and most ambitious work, and might be termed a prose epic rather than a novel.

Tolstoy also planned a novel on the period of Peter the Great, but the more he studied this subject the less he liked it; he found the whole epoch unsympathetic, and declared that Peter's so-called reforms were not really intended for the good of the people, but mainly for his own personal profit, and that what he really desired was freedom for a life of immorality.

Tolstoy's next great novel, *Anna Karénina*, was based on an event which had occurred in real life—the suicide of a young lady who, owing to an unhappy love affair, flung herself before a train. Tolstoy chose as a motto for his book the biblical saying: "Vengeance is mine, I will repay," the fundamental idea being that people have no right to judge others, and that for human relations there is but one law—the law of mercy. Among all Tolstoy's critics Dostoïevsky appears to have been the only one who understood him in this sense; most readers seem to have interpreted the motto in the narrowest possible way as meaning the punishment of Anna for her breach of the marriage vow.

During all this period of literary activity Tolstoy was greatly aided by his wife; she served as his amanuensis, she alone being able to interpret his crabbed and difficult handwriting with its endless corrections, and one of her relatives records that she seven times re-copied the enormous MS. of *War and Peace*.

It was, as he himself tells us, about his fiftieth year that a great change came over Tolstoy. His life had been one of brilliant success; he had achieved great distinction, he had an excellent property, a congenial wife, a happy family, but he became profoundly dissatisfied. Merejkovsky, the most severe of Tolstoy's critics, ascribes this condition mainly to the ebb of vitality natural at his age, and considers it to be, in its origin, essentially physical and egoistic; but Merejkovsky surely forgets the intense interest in moral and religious problems which Tolstoy had always taken even in his youth; in *The Cossacks*, and in *War and Peace*, Tolstoy's heroes are continually searching for "the meaning of life."

The truth would appear to be that Tolstoy, in his youth greatly perplexed by philosophical and religious doubts, had never solved his problems, but had done what so many men do—evaded them by taking refuge in the joys and duties of practical life; but to most really thoughtful natures there comes a crisis when these duties will no longer serve as anodynes, and the old questionings, ten times stronger for their repression, return once more.

This was really the "Sturm und Drang" period of Tolstoy's life; it came unnaturally late, and its severity was proportioned to its delay. In the book entitled *My Confession*, Tolstoy has given a most sincere, graphic, and terrible account of his sufferings at this period. He traces its inception (surely with accuracy!) to the lack of any true religious faith in his youth. He tells how he had momentary gleams of revelation which showed him what a true religion might be, but his faith soon became merely conventional. Moreover, the new scientific materialism was spreading over Russia, and reaching the intellectual *élite* in the schools and colleges; the ceremonial, superstitious religion of the Greek Church, so essentially mediæval in all its methods of thought, could not stand against this dry, scientific determinism. Tolstoy gave way to scepticism and dissipation, and afterwards forgot and buried deep down his longings for a higher life.

After, as we shall see later, a desperate and almost overwhelming struggle, Tolstoy emerged from his darkness convinced that the true faith lay in a literal obedience to the precepts of the Gospel and especially to the Sermon on the Mount. He thought the precepts of the Gospel were realised more completely in the life of the Russian peasants than in that of any other human beings, and, taking their life as his model, he built up his creed: that the great essentials of life are labour and love, that man should be simple, laborious, and kind, that he ought to give more than he receives, to contribute to the common stock more than he takes from it, that he should rejoice in service; in this life he will find health and happiness, and he will not fear death because if he banishes egoism, the loss of his own personality—even to its total extinction—will not appear to him an evil.

This, stated in its essence, is the "solution" at which Tolstoy arrived, and from the year 1879 onwards we find him devoting his life almost entirely to moral and religious teaching.

Taking peasant life always as his model, he himself lived very frugally and simply; he partook only of the plainest food—vegetarian; he dressed like a peasant, he waited upon himself and did the work of his own room, and he "paid" even for this simple sustenance with the labour of his own hands; he worked at haymaking and reaping in the fields, at woodcutting in the woods, and in the winter he made shoes. He spent a portion of each day in manual labour, giving himself appetite to enjoy his simple diet; his temperance and toil kept him strong and vigorous, and he declared that he had as much time as ever to devote to intellectual work. Tolstoy, had, in fact, returned to the passionate and practical faith of the Middle Ages; his life was the life of a mediæval monk when monasticism was at its best—ascetic, laborious, intellectual—but his nineteenth century scepticism had caused him to omit and reject mediæval dogmas and superstitions.

Tolstoy, like so many other religious mystics, wished to yield up his property entirely and strip himself of all worldly goods. It was here that, as with others before him, he came into conflict with his own family.

Another, though a much less reformer of our own time, General Booth, was able to interest all the members of his own family, and to find in them his best and most willing helpers, but he had the advantage of a wife who was, from the beginning, on his side.

Tolstoy was in a different position: the Countess proved herself an admirable wife so long as he devoted himself to adding lustre and aggrandisement to his family; she helped him in the management of his estates, she understood his literary work and gloried in his renown, but further she could not go; she could not comprehend his moral and religious crisis, and her great terror was lest her children should be, in any degree, impoverished. It is painful to hear that at one time she contemplated appealing to the authorities to have her husband declared insane and incapable of managing his own property.

The truth was that Tolstoy's idealism had come in conflict with that maternal egoism which is the dark side of maternal altruism, and one of the strongest forces of the world. This experience helps us to understand the curious bias against maternity which occurs in much of Tolstoy's later work. With regard to this situation Tolstoy ultimately compromised and, in the year 1888, renounced his estates in favour of his family.

He continued to produce religious works: *The Four Gospels Harmonised and Translated*, 1881-2; *My Religion*, 1884; *The Kingdom of God is Within You*, 1893, &c.

Political events in Russia more and more grieved and distressed him. The Revolutionary Executive Committee condemned Alexander II to death, and carried out their sentence. This event shook the whole nation. Tolstoy was horrified by the crime but he profoundly pitied the criminals; he addressed an open letter to the new emperor, Alexander III, imploring him in the name of Christ to forgive the culprits, and declaring that the only way to Russia's salvation lay in following the precepts of Jesus; the other possible methods—cruel repression and liberal reforms—had both been tried and found wanting. No answer was made, and the regicides were put to death.

Throughout Tolstoy's later work we perceive a horror of violence in all its forms, whether legal or illegal: to him all violent death is murder, and, no matter whether it is inflicted by the sentence of revolutionary committees or by the sentence of the law, it is equally criminal.

Tolstoy went for a time to reside in Moscow, and was, more than ever, startled and dismayed by the great contrasts between the extremes of poverty and of wealth.

In 1882 a census was taken; Tolstoy volunteered his help, and was thus enabled to plumb to the very depths the miseries of Moscow. A full account of this census is given in the book entitled *What to Do?* It is a most clear, graphic, and ruthless study of the miseries of poverty and vice; Tolstoy shows with ironic completeness the total insufficiency of charity to compete with the evil, and asks what remedies are possible.

He arrives at the same conclusion as Mr. Bernard Shaw: "What is wrong with the rich is idleness; what is wrong with the poor is poverty."

He shows how the honest and hard-working toiler is defrauded of his comforts because the results of his labour are appropriated to find luxuries for his masters; he shows how the work of the community is distracted from the production of the necessities required by all to luxuries available only for a few and enervating even to them; moreover the rich themselves, corrupted by their idleness, spread corruption around them which disseminates itself through all classes and creates a race of idlers, parasitic upon the labour of others; the analysis of social conditions given in this little book is acute and keen.

Tolstoy found the city too artificial, and returned to the country, where he resumed his simple life. He composed much popular literature; it was printed by a special press in the form of very cheap booklets, which were carried round by pedlars and sold to the people. Tolstoy henceforth regarded his former literary work as bad and selfish, considering it as being in essence a luxury intended for the entertainment of a limited class. His booklets achieved the purpose he had in view; they were greatly loved by the common people, and have penetrated, in the most remarkable way, to every corner of Russia. So great was the demand that each pamphlet was printed in an edition of twenty-four thousand copies, and of most there were five editions in a single year; towards the end of the fourth year the number of copies sold amounted to twelve millions. The first publications were taken from his reading books for children, and included such tales as *The Prisoner of the Caucasia*, *God Sees the Truth*, *Where Love Is God Is*, &c.

It is interesting to note that other distinguished Russian authors have since followed Tolstoy's example. During an illness he wrote *The Power of Darkness*, which was, however, prohibited for a number of years.

In 1891-2 he was occupied in relieving the dreadful Russian famine, procuring assistance by his appeals to Western Europe and, with the money obtained, organising relief-works in different districts.

Tolstoy became greatly interested in the Doukbobors: they were a Russian Nonconformist sect, many of whose principles—condemnation of violence, of taking life and of all church-ritual—were closely akin to his own. They were cruelly persecuted, and Tolstoy did his utmost to aid them; at length they received permission to emigrate to Canada, but were without money for the passage, and, in order to provide it, Tolstoy finished and published his last great novel, *Resurrection*, in 1899; it had been begun some time previously but abandoned.

In March 1901 Tolstoy was formally excommunicated by the Russian Church, as the unorthodox character of his writings and teachings was undeniable, while their great and ever-increasing influence made them too powerful to be ignored.

But this excommunication had the opposite effect to the one intended; the Russian people seemed to awaken suddenly to the fact that this man was indeed their great prophet, and the noblest moral teacher they had ever possessed; he was treated with an ever-growing reverence and sympathy; incessant deputations were sent to express the national admiration.

Tolstoy's influence grew, not only in his own country but abroad: he continued to work at his literary labours, and, even at his death, left a considerable amount of MS. which is still in process of publication. His old age was far from peaceful; the unhappy condition of his country tore his heart.

Silent for long on political matters, the cruel repression of the revolution was too much for him; he published in the leading organs of the European press the mournful and tragic letter beginning, "I can keep silence no longer." He declares that his unhappy country is so given over to crimes of violence, both legal and illegal, that, if men had their way, there would be literally not one human being left uncondemned, but all would perish. He summons all parties, as their only way of salvation, to cease from hatred and revenge, and he tells the Government that, if they must have victims, he offers his "own old throat," as an expiation: but little of his life is left, and that little is made unendurable by the sight of sufferings so terrible.

Tolstoy was also distressed by the luxury of his wife and family; he longed to leave them, but it was against his principles to grieve anyone wilfully. At length, however, he felt that he must have a time of peace for the end. He fled from his home on a snowy autumn night in company with one trusted friend, but the chill and the exposure were too much for him; he was compelled to relinquish his journey at a little wayside station, and he died there in the house of the station-master, a man belonging to the peasant class whom he so loved, and who touchingly and simply received him. The date was November 20, 1910. He was buried on his own estate without, of course, any ceremony from the Church which had repudiated him; the service was conducted mainly by the peasants who had loved him like a father. The Russian Government, which had not dared to touch him, kept over his followers to the last the iron hand of repression; thousands who had wished to attend his funeral were prohibited from doing so; many of his works are still censored, and his disciples still persecuted.

CHAPTER IV

"WAR AND PEACE"

War and Peace is the longest and most important of Tolstoy's single works. In this book Tolstoy aimed at giving the picture of a whole epoch, and that one of the most stirring in the history of modern Europe; the real subject is the conflict between the French and the Prussians from 1805 to 1812, the historical events of the novel concluding with the tragedy of the French retreat from Moscow. The enormous scope of the book, the power of its psychology, the vast number of characters crowding its pages, its tremendous vitality—all won for Tolstoy a recognition deservedly world-wide. After reading it we feel as if we have beheld with our own eyes a terrific and soul-stirring crisis in the history of a great nation, and one of the epoch-making events of the world. And yet the work is truly a novel, and not history in the form of fiction, because we are shown all these events not in the dry, detached light of the historian (whom Tolstoy dislikes), but through their effect on the minds and souls of the private individuals participating in them. Tolstoy selects a little group of Russian families whose circumstances involve them in all the main events; we see with their eyes and hear with their ears; we share in their sufferings, until at the end it is difficult to believe that we ourselves have not witnessed Austerlitz and Borodino, the conflagration of Moscow, and the horrors of the French retreat. Yet the total impression is not one of catastrophe; the great nation, having shed of its heart's blood and sacrificed its noblest, yet recuperates and recovers; those who are left continue the race, and life proceeds as before.

The whole narrative is grouped around three families: the Bolkonskys, the Rostofs, and the Bezukhois, whose relations and inter-relations are very skilfully planned.

The book has three heroes, one in each of the families, and our attention is first attracted to Prince Andrei Bolkonsky. He is a man of high rank, son of a distinguished general, possessed of aristocratic prejudice, handsome, far more intellectual than his companions; the faults of his character are haughtiness and disdain; far superior to the majority of human beings, he is only too keenly conscious of the fact. Yet Prince Andrei is capable of strong and deep affections; he dearly loves his father, his sister, and one friend—Pierre Bezukhoi. Bezukhoi is massive, clumsy, and sensuous, but the keen-sighted Prince Andrei pierces through all his faults and judges his friend justly when he declares that he has "a heart of gold." Among the people whom Prince Andrei secretly despises is his own wife, the Princess Lisa: he finds her cowardly and frivolous, and, though outwardly respectful, he has little real affection.

Prince Andrei enters military service; he becomes aide-de-camp to Kutuzof, and Tolstoy thus has an opportunity of showing us the whole course of the campaign from a really intimate point of view. The great passion of Prince Andrei's life is ambition—the desire for glory—and he considers war as being essentially a means to honour; he is present throughout the battle of Austerlitz, where his calm, cool courage wins him the highest commendations. But the experience changes all his views of life. In the first place he realises how seldom the rewards of courage go to the really deserving.

During the engagement at the Enns the honours of the day really rest with an obscure artillery officer named Tushin, who keeps his battery firing upon the French, and at the critical moment covers the Russian retreat; Tushin's gunners are almost annihilated, but, with the most heroic courage, the battery stick to their task and the army is saved. Tushin himself is a modest and unassuming man, and his superiors are so confused that they not only fail to recognise his achievement, but are about to reprimand him severely for losing some of his guns; Prince Andrei's indignant protest that this man has saved the army spares Tushin the reprimand, but his superiors are too hopelessly bewildered to recognise the truth. The real hero of the day is thus a man who gains nothing—not a single reward or honour—and is only too thankful to escape blame.

At Austerlitz, when the Russian army are broken and in flight, Prince Andrei attempts to save the day; he stems the tide of the fugitives, seizes the flag as it falls from the hand of a dying officer, and leads the whole battalion against a French battery; he is shot down with the flag still in his hand; he believes himself fatally wounded and, as he sinks into unconsciousness, realises suddenly the emptiness of all he has striven for and the beauty of that sweet and profound peace which lies at the heart of the world, but which, until that moment of marvellous insight—-the insight given by the near approach of death—he had never even seen.

"He opened his eyes, hoping to see how the struggle between the artilleryman and the Frenchman ended, and anxious to know whether or not the red-headed artillerist was killed, and the cannon saved or captured. But he could see nothing of it. Over him, he could see nothing except the sky, the lofty sky, no longer clear but still immeasurably lofty and with light grey clouds slowly wandering over it.

"'How still, calm, and solemn! How entirely different from when I was running,' said Prince Andrei to himself. 'It was not so when we were all running and shouting and fighting.... How is it that I never saw before this lofty sky? And how glad I am that I have learned to know it at last. Yes! all is empty, all is deception, except these infinite heavens. Nothing, nothing at all, beside! And even that is nothing but silence and peace! And thank God!'"

Prince Andrei, sinking once more into unconsciousness, recovers to find Napoleon surveying him and calling him "une belle mort." When it is discovered that he is alive Napoleon congratulates him on his magnificent courage; but even the praise of this man, hitherto Prince Andrei's idol, does not move him. He has seen, once and for all, the emptiness of military glory. He recovers from his wound, and, softened and tender, returns to his family, who are mourning him as dead; he finds a son just born to him and his wife dying in childbirth.

Henceforward Prince Andrei is changed, gentle, and tender, but melancholy, and regarding himself as a man whose life is done. Interest returns again when he meets Natasha Rostof—one of the most charming heroines in fiction; Natasha is the very embodiment of joy in life, all poetry, passion, and romance. She enthrals Prince Andrei, he is happy as he has never been, and they are betrothed, but the opposition of his family causes the marriage to be postponed.

Unfortunately Natasha has the defects of her qualities; she allows herself to be fascinated (though only momentarily) by a hopelessly inferior man. Prince Andrei, deeply wounded both in his love and in his pride, refuses to forgive; the old bitterness against life, the old anger return once more. He seeks his rival, Kuragin, and, not finding him, re-enters military service.

At the battle of Borodino Prince Andrei is wounded again, and this time, as it proves, fatally; he lingers for some weeks, and, before his death, fate grants him one last happiness; the Rostofs, in the flight from Moscow, sacrifice their own property to save some Russian wounded among whom, unknown to them, is Prince Andrei; he and Natasha meet again.

In all Tolstoy's pages none are more lovely and pathetic than those depicting this union on the edge of the grave; for a time there is hope—the renewal of his heart's joy assisting the wounded man to rally—but it is only for a brief space, and there succeeds the tragic and terrible yet beautiful alienation of death.

Prince Andrei is one of the few Tolstoyan heroes who have no physical fear of death, who meet it, not with shuddering nausea, but with noble and grave composure. If he clings to life it is not from any weak fear but because life means Natasha, poetry, and joy; when the pang of resignation is once over, all is peace.

"Prince Andrei not only knew that he was going to die, but he also felt that he was dying, that he was already half-way towards death. He experienced a consciousness of alienation from everything earthly, and a strange beatific exaltation of being. Without impatience and without anxiety, he waited for what was before him. That ominous Eternal Presence, unknown and far away, which had never once ceased, throughout all his life, to haunt his senses, was now near at hand and, by reason of that strange exhilaration which he felt, almost comprehensible and palpable."

Natasha and his sister grieve for themselves, but they cannot really grieve for him. "They both saw how he was sinking, deeper and deeper, slowly and peacefully away from them, and they both knew that this was inevitable, and that it was well. He was shrived and partook of the sacrament. All came to bid him farewell.

"When his little son was brought, he kissed him and turned away, not because his heart was sore and filled with pity, but simply because this was all that was required of him."

In this lofty and beautiful isolation the hero passes away. Prince Andrei has something in him of Byronism; there is the Byronic ideal in his aristocratic disdain, his mental solitude, his melancholy; he is Byronic also in his courage, his love of glory and his disillusionment with glory, but no mere Byronist could ever have drawn the portrait. The marvellous thing in Tolstoy's art is that he so plainly reveals the change and development of human character; we never feel that his people are static and finished; before our very eyes Prince Andrei changes from Byronic pride to sweetness and tenderness, a bitter disillusion brings him back to pride, but, once more, the depths of the man's nature are stirred and his fundamental sweetness is revealed.

Many times in his epic novel Tolstoy makes us feel the bitter cost of war, but never more than in the death of this, the noblest of his heroes, on the threshold of happiness and love.

Pierre Bezukhoi—the second hero—is a wholly different type. He is much more Russian and national than Prince Andrei; the two are so unlike that the friendship between them strikes us with the same surprise as it would in real life. Pierre is clumsy and awkward, and not sufficiently strong-willed; he is continually led away to do things he does not desire; his chief fault is sensuality, and this is the rock on which he all but wrecks his life. It leads him into marriage with a woman whom he desires but does not love—the beautiful, profligate Elena. The analysis of his motives is wrought with a terrible sombre power, which anticipates *The Kreutzer Sonata*. Pierre, in the toils of his own sensuality, is, on our first acquaintance with him, a most unattractive character, and we wonder why Tolstoy has allowed him a position so prominent, just as we wonder why the fastidious Prince Andrei can have selected him as a friend; but, by degrees, we realise his true nature; he has indeed a heart of gold and, little by little, his goodness and kindness and simplicity shake his character free from its coarsest faults. He has a genius for sympathy, and he appears to understand all those who surround him better than they understand themselves. The real love of his life is Natasha Rostof, but he does his best, most unselfishly, to reconcile her to Prince Andrei; in a sense he deserves her the better of the two, for, even when her betrothed turns against her, Pierre still loves and appreciates, and his devotion helps her through the darkest hours of her life. It is only fitting that, in the end, Natasha should make him happy. Like Prince Andrei, Pierre finds his moral regeneration in war, but in a different way; he does not enter active service nor is he wounded, but he views other aspects of the great tragedy; he is present at the burning of Moscow, he is captured by the French, and taken as prisoner on their terrible retreat. It is the heroism of the common man, the beauty and nobility of suffering finely borne, which redeem Pierre from the depression which has darkened his mind and which teach him the true meaning of life.

He is especially influenced by one man—the peasant soldier Platon Karatayef—one of Tolstoy's greatest creations. Platon is not clever nor handsome, his whole life has been privation, but he is love itself, kind and sweet to all men. Most tragic is his fate! The French shoot those of the Russian prisoners who cannot keep up with the march, and Pierre, seeing his friend failing, cannot endure the thought of what must happen and keeps away. One morning he sees Platon, not attempting to walk, but sitting beneath a tree with a calm and radiantly happy expression; he gives a beseeching glance to Pierre, but Pierre turns his back and walks off. Shortly afterwards there is heard the sound of a gunshot, two French soldiers pass with guilty faces, and there is the melancholy howling of Karatayef's dog.

Platon's fate is one of the means Tolstoy uses to drive home his lesson of the immense futility of war; it is to the last degree abominable that this most loving and beautiful nature, wholly guiltless, should be murdered in cold blood; even a dog has the sense to lament such a deed.

But the moral of this wonderful nature is not lost upon Pierre; he finds in it "the meaning of life," the clue which he has all along been seeking. As Pierre's sufferings increase so does his heart grow lighter; he learns the joy of endurance and the pleasure even of anguish, and all things are less grievous than he would have thought.

"Of all that which he afterwards called sufferings, but which at the time he scarcely felt, the worst was from his bare, bruised, scurvy-scarred feet. The horse-flesh was palatable and nourishing, the saltpetre odour of the gunpowder which they used instead of salt was even pleasant ... the vermin which fed upon him warmed his body. The one thing hard at that time was the state of his feet. On the second day of the retreat, Pierre, examining his sores by the fire, felt that it was impossible to take another step on them; but when all got up he went along, treading gingerly, and afterwards, when he was warmed to it, he walked without pain, though when evening came it was more than ever terrible to look at his feet. But he did not look at them and turned his thoughts to other things.... He saw and heard not how the prisoners who straggled were shot down, although more than a hundred had perished in this way.... The more trying his position, the more appalling the future, ... the more joyful and consoling were the thoughts, recollections, and visions which came to him."

Tolstoy's account of this terrible retreat is Homeric in its tragic nobility; Homeric, too, is the spirit of the Russian army: they are short of food, short of clothes, sleeping in the snow at twenty degrees below zero; they melt away to half their numbers, yet they grow ever happier and happier, more and more cheerful, for all the poor-spirited, the weak, and cowardly succumb, and only the heroes remain. In his previous life Pierre has been miserable, disenchanted, and disillusioned, but he emerges from this hell of suffering a man finally happy. And Tolstoy makes us see that it could not be otherwise; his hero has learnt for ever the tremendous capacities of the human soul.

Of Tolstoy's two heroines the Princess Mariya is the nobler type; she is what he imagined his mother to have been, and to this, no doubt, a large part of her fascination may be traced. In her the author has drawn a woman exceedingly plain, not particularly clever, without accomplishments and melancholy by temperament, yet, by sheer spiritual beauty, she compels admiration, affection, even passionate love.

Her physical appearance, on which Tolstoy dwells, gives the clue to her nature; she treads heavily and blushes unbecomingly in patches; this heavy tread shows us her awkwardness and self-distrust, and the blushing her almost painful modesty.

But she is one of those who have life's secret—the gift of love; she idolises her brother; she loves and admires her little selfish sister-in-law, the Princess Lisa; she bears, year in and year out, with the exasperating and even cruel tyrannies of her father, and loves him dearly to the end; she cherishes her nephew. Ultimately, though slowly, she wins her reward for all this patient sweetness; her brother has always understood her at her full value, her father dies acknowledging her as his good angel, and we are not surprised when Nikolai Rostof, cold to more beautiful and more attractive women, turns and gives her his love.

And yet the portrait is not sentimentalised or made incredibly virtuous; the Princess Mariya does not find self-abnegation easy, she longs for a home and happiness, she is jealous of Natasha because Natasha is young and beautiful, and has achieved the poetry of love; to the end, notwithstanding her deep affections, she finds it a little hard to comprehend others.

Tolstoy's second heroine, Natasha Rostof, is, for pure fascination, the most enthralling character in the book. Tolstoy seems to have drawn her from an actual person—his sister-in-law; and she has all the reality of a minute portrait.

Natasha is beautiful or, it would be more correct to say, has the promise of beauty; she has also a lovely voice; but her most remarkable gift is her power of winning love. From her first introduction she is the idolised of all; she and her younger brother, Petya, are her mother's favourite children; Natasha is the adored of her brothers and her father, and almost every man who visits the house falls in love with her. Tolstoy makes us understand why. Natasha is herself prepared to see all that is delightful and all that is good in others; she is highly vitalised; she has strong affections, and an intense joy in life; wherever Natasha is things move; it is she who is always ready to suggest games and amusements; it is she who perceives poetry and romance where others cannot or only in much less degree. Morning in the forest, a moonlight night in spring, sledging over the snow, music—all are to her enrapturing things. That magical period of youth, that period of half-childhood, half-adolescence, when the world is suffused by "the light that never was on sea or land," has nowhere been more beautifully depicted than in her. It is this romantic charm which so powerfully attracts the somewhat cold but poetic nature of Prince Andrei. In the midst of the gloomy tragedies of bloodshed and battle Natasha Rostof shines like an incarnation of springtime, the very joy of life in a human form. The most beautiful passage in the whole novel is probably that which describes Prince Andrei's first meeting with her.

He is in a mood of some sadness, and feels, after all his experiences, old beyond his years; he drives to the Rostofs and perceives a number of young girls running among the trees. "In front of the others ... ran a very slender, indeed a strangely slender maiden, with dark hair and dark eyes, in a yellow chintz dress, with a white handkerchief round her head, the locks emerging from it in ringlets."

It is Natasha, and, that same night, Prince Andrei hears her conversing with her cousin Sonya at the window above his own. "The night was cool and calmly beautiful. In front of the window was a row of clipped trees, dark on one side and silver-bright on the other.... Farther away, beyond the trees, was a roof glittering with dew; farther to the right a tall tree with wide-spreading branches, showed a brilliant white bole and limbs; and directly above it the moon, almost at her full, shone in the bright, nearly starless spring night. Prince Andrei leaned his elbows on the window-sill and fixed his eyes on that sky."

He hears Sonya and Natasha sing a duet, he hears Sonya try to persuade her cousin to sleep and Natasha's protest:

"Sonya! Sonya! How can you go to sleep? Just see how lovely it is! How lovely! Come wake up, Sonya," she said again with, tears in her voice. "Come, now, such a lovely, lovely night was never seen!"

Prince Andrei meets her again at a ball in St. Petersburg, where her childlike happiness brings a breath of pure air into the artificial atmosphere; Natasha is so completely unaffected that, in the very midst of affectations, she keeps her unspoilt romance.

Prince Andrei proposes for her hand, but the Rostofs' family affairs are in confusion, and Prince Andrei's father insists on a year's delay; for that space of time he goes abroad. Prince Andrei does not find the time of delay unreasonably long, and cannot understand that Natasha should do so, but the girl suffers the dangers of her inexperience; Prince Andrei has roused her to a full consciousness of womanhood, and her sensuous and passionate nature cannot endure the blank of his absence; also, since she is extremely sensitive, she is grieved by the cold attitude his family persistently maintain.

She meets Anatol Kuragin, a man exceedingly handsome but unscrupulous, who at once makes violent love to her; she writes a letter to Prince Andrei breaking off their engagement, and consents to elope with Kuragin, this plan being discovered and frustrated by her family. Natasha wakens from her brief madness, realises how badly she has behaved to her betrothed, and, in her remorse and shame, attempts suicide.

Prince Andrei, returning, learns the whole story; he is stung to the quick in his haughty pride; his spiritual nature makes him totally unable to understand the temptation, and he cannot forgive.

It is Natasha's innate generosity which gives them, however, their last chance of reconciliation; the Rostofs are carting their family property away from Moscow, which is threatened by the French, but there are not sufficient horses to transport the Russian wounded, and Natasha, keenly opposing her mother, demands that the family property shall be sacrificed, and the wounded rescued instead; the Rostofs discover Prince Andrei's presence and forbid Natasha to see him, but her own daring takes her to his side, and there follows the most simple but touching of reconciliations.

Natasha becomes his nurse, and proves the depth of her nature by her skill and tenderness. But the brief time of joy is soon over; Prince Andrei's sufferings are agonising, and he passes away.

Natasha feels bereavement with the same intensity as everything else; she herself seems to sink out of the world; thin and pale and visibly wasting away, she sits for hours in silence, gazing at the place where Prince Andrei has lain. Her family have lost all hope of saving her life, but tragic news arrives; the younger brother—Petya—has been killed in battle, and the mother is mad with grief; she screams for her beloved Natasha, who is the only person who can comfort her, and, in straining every nerve to save her mother's reason, the girl herself is restored to life. She lives again by virtue of those profound and passionate affections which had almost destroyed her. She is so greatly changed, however, that, when Pierre meets her again, he does not know her; he cannot recognise in her thin, pale, and stern face the Natasha of adorable and abounding life; yet the moment he shows that he loves her, the old Natasha, with her radiant joy, flashes back into his view, and she is willing, almost at once, to become Pierre's affianced. To the Princess Mariya, with a nature much less emotional but infinitely more constant, Natasha is a continual marvel, and, though she is glad of her friend's happiness, the Princess grieves at the inconstancy to her brother.

The whole portrait is wonderful in its realism, glowing with vitality and with charm, and, just as in the case of the men, Natasha deepens and changes before our very eyes.

But few readers will be inclined, however, to appreciate Tolstoy's final picture of her; he shows us Natasha as Pierre's wife and the mother of four children; she is loving but exacting, very jealous, almost parsimonious in her care for her children, she has become untidy in her personal appearance, and the old poetic charm only in the rarest moments returns.

Natasha, in fact, seems to show us the limitations in Tolstoy's patriarchal view of woman; he regards her not really as an individual, an end in herself, but as a means towards the race, and the individual loss is nothing to regret; he seems to realise and rejoice in the shock he gives us when he tells us of Natasha the generous become parsimonious, of Natasha the sylph tearing round in a dirty morning wrapper; but we are inclined to resent the admiration accorded to this second Natasha, who limits her sympathies to such a narrow circle, and who has become a maternal egoist of the most colossal type. Tolstoy himself found, as we have seen, in his relations with his wife, that the maternal egoist is not quite the finest ideal of humanity.

It is impossible to study in any detail the crowded canvas of *War and Peace,* but the minor characters are often among the best-drawn and the most attractive.

The whole Rostof group are delightfully depicted. Petya Rostof, the dear boy who is killed, has almost the same charm as Natasha. He has intense affections, is full of amusing boyish interests, and possesses a lofty ideal of patriotism; he likes to think himself a hero, and really is one. When only sixteen he insists on joining the army: his brother's friends try to protect him and to keep him out of danger, but his gallantry leads him into every peril, and he is killed, quite uselessly and casually, while exposing himself in a dangerous engagement. It is one more example of the immense futility of war. Nikolai Rostof, Tolstoy's third hero, is more commonplace than Pierre and Prince Andrei, but he gives Tolstoy a splendid opportunity for depicting the psychology of war; we are shown all his emotions from the day when he first joins, is alternately elated with a feeling of heroism and depressed by the conviction that he is a coward, to the time when, as a seasoned veteran, he can hardly recall his old excitement and his old dread; the only trace his former fear has left in his mind shows itself in his compassion for the younger officers, whose mental sufferings he so fully understands. Nikolai Rostof has always a certain humility of character; he is very ready to reverence others, and is attracted to the Princess Mariya by her great spiritual superiority to himself.

The artillery officer, Tushin, to whom we have already alluded, is evidently Tolstoy's type of a true Russian hero. He is simplicity and modesty itself; his magnificent courage is not in the least sanguinary, but is accompanied by a heart as tender as a woman's; when he is returning after his terrific day he is still kind enough to help the wounded Nikolai Rostof on to the blood-bespattered gun-carriage.

Nor does Tushin stand alone; continually in *War and Peace*, as in so many other works, Tolstoy makes us feel the enormous value of man as man.

With the really eminent we cannot but feel that he is less successful. One curious feature of the book is its almost Eastern fatalism. Tolstoy will allow practically nothing to the will of man as an individual; all the great events of the book are due to the power of an unknown destiny urging men on to deeds which are, even to themselves, unexpected and surprising, while the men who think that they are directing all are really as helplessly incapable of any true control as a fly revolving upon a cart-wheel.

Tolstoy is especially embittered towards Napoleon; he does not blame him, like Byron, because his greatness was "antithetically mixed" with so much of meanness; he does not blame him, like Shelley, because, possessing in his genius a unique opportunity for good, he chose to divert that genius to his own self-aggrandisement.

Tolstoy goes much further; he is so excessively angry that he altogether denies Napoleon's genius; he will not acknowledge him to have any talent except of the most trifling kind; to him Napoleon is a mean-souled, small-minded man, contemptible in everything, colossal in his vanity but great in nothing besides. And when the reader asks in amazement how Napoleon won his tremendous victories, how he gained the unparalleled devotion of his army, Tolstoy answers contemptuously that the victories were due mainly to destiny, to the unknown Ruler of the world who so ordained, and that the devotion of the army was mere hypnotism. Nor is it only from Napoleon that he endeavours to strip the borrowed plumes; in several amusing studies Napoleon's great soldier-marshals are revealed as vain, childish, and even absurd, proud of their uniforms and almost infantile in their love of decorations. But, it must be confessed, Tolstoy is impartial in his dislike of the eminent; he is almost as hard on the Russian generals as on the French. The one man whom he praises—Kutuzof—is the man whom the Russians themselves failed to appreciate, and Tolstoy admires him for the somewhat curious reason that he also was a fatalist, that he believed no general could do much, and was always, with Fabian tactics, waiting upon the event.

CHAPTER V

"ANNA KARÉNINA"

Anna Karénina is, perhaps, considered as a whole, a more artistic work than *War and Peace*; the very fact that its scope is less gigantic permits Tolstoy to make it clearer and more concentrated; everything is directed towards the one end—the tragic death of Anna—and though the novel has an under-plot, that is very skilfully blent with the main plot, and is everywhere kept subordinate.

Anna Karénina is much less distinctively Russian and national than *War and Peace*; it shows very plainly the influence of the French novel, and its plot is of the type that French novelists are fond of selecting, though the moral intensity with which Tolstoy invests it is unusual with them.

Notwithstanding the power and beauty of its telling, it seems, however, somewhat restricted when compared with the vast spaces and terrific issues of *War and Peace*, where individual tragedies, however great, are forgotten in the crisis of a nation.

Anna Karénina is a very great novel, but no one would dream of saying that it suggested Homer. It is a domestic tragedy only, but, like Shakespeare in *Othello*, Tolstoy has known how to make his domestic tragedy a revelation of the heights and depths, of the passionate potentialities of the human soul.

Tolstoy openly refrains from judging his heroine, and it is a mistake to consider *Anna Karénina* as being essentially a protest against the breaking of the marriage bond. Tolstoy does believe in the indissolubility of marriage, but the book is just as much a protest against the dangers of marriage without love or the cruel injustice of society.

The truth is that it is a picture of life, and expresses, as Tolstoy acutely says an artistic work always should, a moral relation to life rather than a moral judgment.

Anna Karénina, is, of all Tolstoy's heroines, the most perfect human being; she is a mature woman, possessed of wit, grace, and beauty, and above all, the gift of sympathy; she is one of those people who have strong affections, who love profoundly and appreciate readily all that is best in others, who are also possessed of keen intellectual powers, but who live mainly from impulse and not from principle. Such people are, perhaps, the most attractive characters in the world, and their impulses, springing from a warm heart, are usually right: but it is their peril that, in moments of moral stress, their emotions may be too much for them, and may fatally mislead them. There is a certain resemblance, though not too close, between Anna and Natasha Rostof; both possess the poetic and emotional temperament; they add, wherever they are, to the romance of life; it may be noted too that, though Natasha's fate is happier, that is due mainly to accident, and not to her own achievement, for she twice escaped the ruin of her life only by the intervention of others, and she also came very near to death by her own hand.

There is no surer proof of Anna's sweetness than the charm she possesses for members of her own sex. She appreciates the beauty of the young girl who is her unconscious rival, Kitty Shcherbatsky, and she can enter into the family griefs and troubles of Kitty's sister Dolly, who, although most virtuous herself, clings to Anna through all her ostracism. Even the frivolous and immoral Betsky Tverskáia is grieved to the heart when her own cowardice compels her to desert Anna.

Even before the heroine enters the story the effect of her presence is felt. Her brother who, owing to a matrimonial infidelity, has quarrelled with his wife, looks to her as his only hope; he and Dolly both love her dearly, and they hope that she may find for them a way out of the intolerable situation; she does, in fact, prevent the break-up of the home, though she cannot (and this is another example of Tolstoy's quiet ironic truth) either reform her brother or leave Dolly really happy. Tender and sympathetic as Anna at once shows herself to be, she has yet a void in her own life. When quite a young girl she had been married to a government official, Aleksei Karénin, who held an important position but who was twenty years her senior, stiff, dry, and cold; the marriage was entirely due to the intrigues of Anna's clever and unscrupulous aunt.

Anna has one child, her son Serozha, and in the effort to fill her life completely with her maternal affection, she has almost made it an affectation. Though she herself hardly suspects it, the real emotional capacities of her nature have never been developed. It is a stroke of tragic irony that Anna, who comes to Moscow to avert the destruction of her brother's home, should find there what is to prove the ruin of her own. She meets Count Aleksei Vronsky—young, handsome, attractive.

Vronsky has been regarded by everyone, including Kitty herself, as the suitor of Kitty Shcherbatsky, but he is not deeply stirred, and, the moment he meets Anna, he yields to her far greater charm.

Had there been the slightest disrespect in Vronsky's attentions, Anna would have known how to defend herself, but Vronsky is perfectly reverent. His family, on discovering the intrigue, consider Anna simply as an amusement for Vronsky, but he himself has never regarded her in that light; from the first moment he has loved her seriously and profoundly, with all the strength of his nature.

Against all the ordinary infidelities, the light and cheap loves of the society in which she lives, Anna is immune, but she is helplessly ensnared by this love, so immediate that she has no time to be on her guard, so tender and reverent that she cannot feel insulted.

The reader is, at first, somewhat inclined to resent Anna's overwhelming passion, and to consider Vronsky as commonplace, he seems so much the typical military dandy, his whole life's aim (as he avows even to himself) being the desire to be *comme il faut* in everything—in dress, speech, manners, and sentiments. He attempts to make his passion for Madame Karénina fit in the conventional framework, but Vronsky is finer than he himself suspects; he really is what Anna had, at the first glimpse, divined him to be—her nature's destined mate; under the exterior of the St. Petersburg dandy, he conceals a nature capable of extraordinary generosities and the most enduring devotion. He realises all the charm of Anna's nature; he realises that her heart is as yet unawakened and that he has the power to arouse it; there is nothing in his moral code to hold him back; he and his society consider the pursuit of a married woman as being quite *comme il faut*. Our first real surprise with regard to Vronsky does not occur in his relations to Anna, but comes when we discover that he has, with almost quixotic generosity, sacrificed the greater part of his fortune in favour of his younger brother, for no reason except that his brother wished to marry into a distinguished family, and the fortune would greatly aid.

With the same generosity, Vronsky, when he discovers the need, makes real sacrifices for Anna. He had at first regarded his passion for her as being only an additional joy in life, entailing no responsibility; but Tolstoy, with his unerring accuracy, shows that the responsibilities of an illicit love are not only as great as those of a legal one, but far more difficult and galling, because society, having ordained the responsibilities of marriage, assists the individual to execute them, whereas, in the other case, it incessantly hinders and impedes. Vronsky is compelled either to leave Anna or to sacrifice his ambition, hitherto the dearest thing in his life, and he gives up his ambition.

Matthew Arnold, in his criticisms on *Anna Karénina*, remarks that it is difficult to imagine an Englishwoman yielding herself as readily as Anna to an illicit love. But we may doubt if this is not a piece of British Pharasaism, for an emotional Englishwoman, living in a society as corrupt as Anna's (and many periods of English society have been as corrupt), would probably yield in the same way. Tolstoy, with his usual insight, has shown us how natural this yielding really is. Anna, though quite young, is well accustomed to marital infidelity; her own brother's, though it distresses, does not shock her; moreover, in the character of this brother, Stepan, we have a subtle side-light thrown upon Anna's; Stepan is a far inferior type, but there is undoubtedly a family affinity. Stepan is affectionate, kind-hearted, and cheerful; wherever he goes he is thoroughly liked; but he altogether fails to realise his obligations, even to those he loves, and in Anna's nature, incomparably more refined, there is, none the less, a touch of the same carelessness.

Anna's husband is not the person to exercise any restraining influence. Tolstoy never agrees with the wife's conception of him as a mere official machine, but he makes us understand how inevitable it is that Anna should take such a view. Karénin is cold by nature, and, in her sense of the word, he has never really loved her; her relations with Vronsky do not so much wound and grieve his affections (Anna could readily understand that), but they fill him with an overmastering fear for his dignity, his place in society, and, to an idealist like Anna, this very fear appears as contemptible.

The course of the long, ever-changing drama between these three is traced with acutest psychological skill. Anna yields to her lover only after long solicitation, and with an instant shame and regret; for a time she hides the truth from

Karénin, but concealment of any sort is hateful to her candour, and soon becomes impossible; she is present at a dangerous steeple-chase when Vronsky is thrown, and her emotion is so manifest that her husband rebukes her; she gives way to her own passionate desire for truth, and, notwithstanding her bitter humiliation, acknowledges her infidelity. She hopes that the confession will end an intolerable situation, but her hope is disappointed; her husband simply forbids her to receive Vronsky in his house, and Anna finds that one insufferable situation has only given place to another still worse; to deceive Karénin was a torture, but to live on terms of cold hostility with him, seeing her lover by stealth, is even more wretched. Karénin meditates a divorce, but neither Anna nor he really desires it; he cannot bear to yield her entirely to Vronsky, and Anna knows that it would mean a final separation from her son. In the meantime Vronsky is sacrificing his whole career in order to remain in St. Petersburg. Anna longs for death, and nature seems about to send it; her daughter—Vronsky's child—is born, and for a week she hangs between life and death. In her extremity her mind is oppressed by remorse for the suffering she has caused her husband; she entreats his forgiveness, and with great compassion he does, really and genuinely, forgive; he even consents to be reconciled to Vronsky, and, at Anna's bedside, they clasp hands.

But destiny reveals its customary irony (Tolstoy, we may remark, is as firm a believer in tragic irony as any of the Greeks). The touching reconciliation is based really upon one condition—that Anna dies—and this does not happen. Moreover she, who had, for a moment, exalted her husband above her lover, soon finds the balance redressed. Vronsky discovers himself in a position for which his philosophy has no remedy; instead of being the triumphant lover he finds himself a humiliated offender, pardoned by the man whom he had most grievously injured; there was also the terrible anguish of believing Anna's death inevitable. Vronsky shoots himself, bungles it, and is wounded seriously though not fatally. His attempted suicide is, in part, a supreme sacrifice to his doctrine of *comme il faut*, an attempt to escape humiliation and ridicule, in part a manifestation of the feeling, so strong it amazes even himself, that life without Anna is impossible.

But Anna recovers; Vronsky's attempted suicide has turned her sympathies almost wholly to him, and when once she is convalescent (here again is the tragic irony) she finds her husband as tiresome and tedious as before.

Vronsky and Anna end the intolerable situation by taking flight. For a time all seems well with them; after so many brief and stolen interviews, so many harsh separations, they find it unalloyed bliss to be together without let or hindrance; they spend in Italy an ideally happy honeymoon.

But Tolstoy's art is inexorable, as inexorable as life.

Neither Vronsky nor Anna can remain content in isolation; they are both rich and generous natures, meant for fruitful intercourse with their fellows, and they cannot, in their position, obtain either suitable society or suitable duties. Vronsky has resigned his military profession, which he really loved, and for which he was admirably adapted; he does his best to find occupation in other ways; in Italy he attempts art, but soon discovers that he is a mere dilettante, wasting his efforts and his time. They return to Russia, and he devotes himself to the duties of a landed proprietor, becoming quite reasonably successful. So far as he himself is concerned Vronsky could get along, but he is stabbed through his affection for Anna; the really intolerable burden of the situation falls upon her; men will associate with her, but not her own sex; she is ostracised from the society of good women, and even women who are, morally speaking, infinitely her inferiors venture to insult her; moreover she knows that Vronsky's mother tries to entice him away from her and get him married; she has had to resign her son, and the thought of his destiny, misunderstood, and perhaps neglected, tortures and grieves her. She attempts to obtain a divorce from Karénin, so that her position can be regularised, but her husband, fallen under the sway of a malevolent woman, refuses.

Thrown, as she is, entirely upon Vronsky's honour, she is desperately jealous; every hour that he spends away from her is an anguish, and she is continually tortured by the fear of desertion; conscious that her jealousy exasperates and alienates him, she is still unable to control it.

Vronsky is really a gentleman, and he has true and deep love; he shows great consideration, but the incessant scenes of jealousy followed by passion and passion followed by jealousy strain his patience to the breaking-point. At length, having tried, as he thinks, everything else, he believes that the only way left is to try indifference; Anna, however, is on the edge of the abyss, and his coldness drives her over.

Vronsky is absent for the day; in terror at her own despair she sends him a note, beseeching him to return; he answers coldly that he will be back at the appointed time, and, yielding to her anguish, she flings herself beneath a train.

All Anna's feelings at this crisis of her fate are depicted with the deepest truth and tragedy. The unhappy creature herself knows whither she is tending, and struggles frantically, but her views of life grow ever more and more gloomy; hatred of herself, hatred of her lover, well up in her heart, and, at last, her only desire is to punish him.

"'There,' she said, looking at the shadow of the carriage thrown upon the black coal-dust which covered the sleepers, 'there, in the centre, he will be punished and I shall be delivered from it all ... and from myself.'

"Her little red travelling-bag caused her to miss the moment when she could throw herself under the wheels of the first carriage, as she was unable to detach it from her arm. She awaited the second. A feeling like that she had once experienced just before taking a dive in the river came over her, and she made the sign of the cross. This familiar action awakened in her soul a crowd of memories of youth and childhood. Life, with its elusive joys, glowed for an instant before her, but she did not remove her eyes from the carriage, and when the centre part, between the wheels, appeared, she threw away her red bag, lowered her head upon her shoulders, and, with outstretched hands, threw herself on her knees beneath the vehicle, as though prepared to rise again. She had time to feel afraid. 'Where am I? What am I doing? Why?' thought she, trying to draw back; but a great inflexible mass struck her head and threw her on her back. 'Lord! forgive me all,' she murmured, feeling the struggle to be in vain. A little muzhik, who was mumbling in his beard, leant from the step of the carriage on to the line.

"And the light—which, for the unfortunate one, had lit up the book of life with its troubles, its deceptions, and its pains—rending the darkness, shone with greater brightness, then flickered, grew faint, and went out for ever."

On Vronsky the terrible punishment takes effect; he rejoins the service a crushed and broken man, having henceforward only one desire—to lose his life in battle.

Mingled with the main story of Anna and Vronsky is the companion one or "under-plot" of Kitty Shcherbatsky and Konstantin Levin. We may notice that Tolstoy's method of construction differs essentially from that of Turgénief; Turgénief, making his work briefer and more concentrated, omits all that is not essential to his main theme, but Tolstoy aims at giving, not so much the drama of life as life itself.

He wishes to show us the slow, deliberate motion of reality, and when in Anna's life there are no events, he fills up the space with the acts and experiences of his other characters.

Kitty Shcherbatsky's story is very simple: she at first refuses Levin, believing herself in love with Vronsky; he, however, deserts her for Anna; she is cruelly mortified, passes through a period of ill-health and depression, but Levin ultimately returns, she marries him, and they are happy. Kitty is a charming girl, but her character seems slight and even common-place beside the depth and richness and passion of Anna's; the two heroines in this book do not balance so well as in *War and Peace*, though Tolstoy has most skilfully used them as foils to each other, and helped, by their mutual relations, to reveal their characters; thus there is no stronger proof of Anna's wonderful charm than the fact that Kitty, who has hated her, both from jealousy and because she thinks her wicked, has only to meet her in order to be overwhelmed by love and compassion. Konstantin Levin, is, in some ways, more interesting than Vronsky; he has a much more complex mental development. It is agreed that Levin represents, to some extent, Tolstoy himself. The points of resemblance are many and close; Levin works among his peasants just as Tolstoy did, mowing and reaping in the fields, rejoicing in the health and activity of such a life, and in the lovely pictures of nature that it reveals. Levin's proposal to his wife follows, detail by detail, Tolstoy's proposal to Sophie Behrs; the death of Levin's brother from consumption is like the death of Tolstoy's—even the name is the same—Nicolas; Levin, like Tolstoy, is happy in his family life, but is, nevertheless, so greatly distressed by religious doubts and difficulties that he is driven almost to suicide.

The resemblance being so strong, it is noteworthy and significant that Tolstoy has painted Levin as a great egoist. He is a good fellow at heart, and the reader is thoroughly interested in his mental development, but his egoism is so strong that it continually exasperates and annoys. When Kitty refuses him, Levin is deeply wounded in his affections, but still more hurt in his pride; he cannot get over the fact that he—Levin—has been "refused by a Shcherbatsky," and feels as if the whole world must be cognisant of his disgrace—in fact he becomes really comic. Again, when he hears from her sister that Kitty's affection for Vronsky was really very slight, that her only real regret is the alienation from him, he will not even call at the house, and this though he knows that the whole Vronsky entanglement was due mainly to his own eccentric behaviour. Even when he is married he is incessantly and unnecessarily jealous of his wife, and always, on the slightest pretext, tormenting her with this jealousy.

This irritable self-consciousness is shown no less strikingly in his relations with men who, although they esteem his integrity and talents, find it exceedingly difficult to like him. The same self-consciousness makes him clumsy in society, and, when he has to act with other people in public business, he grows caustic and angry because they do not agree with him in everything. The worst egoism of all occurs in his attitude towards his dying brother. When he sees his brother visibly perishing from consumption, he pities him deeply, but, none the less, his chief concern lies in the thought that this horrible and degrading misfortune of illness and death will one day befall himself; he positively disturbs the invalid in the night (how terrible to break that hard-won sleep of the consumptive!) by rising to look in the glass, dreading to find that he has wrinkles and grey hairs and is growing old.

When he and Kitty attend Nikolai's death-bed we see the strongest possible contrast between the unselfish courage of the young wife, thinking only of the sick man, and doing everything possible for him, and the distressing egoism of Levin, who is filled with fear, disgust, and almost anger at the sight of death.

"Levin, though terrified at the thought of lifting this frightful body under the coverlet, submitted to his wife's influence, and put his arms around the invalid, with that resolute air she knew so well": and again, "The sight of the sick man paralysed him; he did not know what to say, how to look or move about.... Kitty apparently did not think about herself, and she had not the time. Occupied only with the invalid, she seemed to have a clear idea of what to do; and she succeeded in her endeavour."

Anna Karénina shows already that fear of death which is such an obsession in Tolstoy's later works. In *War and Peace*, he takes the soldier's view of it, as something almost trifling in comparison with greater matters; his noble Prince Andrei grieves over many things, but neither the utmost extremity of peril, nor the anguish of his gangrened wound, nor the immediate presence of dissolution can shake his courage or dismay his soul. It is different with the pitiful, almost animal terror of death shown by poor Nikolai Levin, and it plays an increasing part in Tolstoy's mind until, as he describes in *My Confession*, it becomes an obsession which occupies the whole of his mind, and from which he can only shake himself free by an entire conversion. Even then, like a mediæval monk, he allows the thought of death to colour almost the whole of life. The truth is that he thinks too much of it. Even his pagan Homer might have taught him better; Achilles cries:

"My friend, thou too must die; why thus lamentest thou? Patroklos too is dead, who was better far than thou. Seest thou not also what manner of man am I for might and goodliness? and a good man was my father and a goddess-mother bare me. Yet over me too hang death and forceful fate."

Tolstoy had reached, more than once, the height of the heroic age. It is a pity his soul ever condescended to our modern and craven fear of death.

The canvas of *Anna Karénina* is rich in minor characters, almost as excellently drawn as the main one. Stepan, Anna's brother, has been already referred to; he is an ironically complete portrait of the man of the world, drawn with a Thackerayan lightness and zest. There are not, as a rule, many resemblances between Thackeray and Tolstoy, for Tolstoy is so much the deeper, but the portrait of Stepan might have come from the same pen as that of Major Pendennis. Stepan is always kind, but his kindness is as purely constitutional as a good digestion. He is faithless to his wife, not once nor twice, but habitually; he deserts the "adorable" women who confide themselves to his protection; he claims an excellent post, and thinks he has fulfilled all its duties by keeping himself invariably well-dressed; he is, of course, a *connoisseur* in meats and wines, and, however well-spread the table may be, must always show his fastidiousness by ordering something else. He is very generous, and pays all his debts of honour, but the money for this has to be found by his unfortunate family, who economise even in the necessities of life; one summer they spend their time in a miserable tumble-down house; next year, as the place is positively uninhabitable, they are driven to take refuge with the Levins. But it does not grieve Stepan that Konstantin Levin should support Stepan's wife and six children; he doubtless thinks that Levin enjoys that sort of thing as much as he—Stepan—the spending of money. Yet Stepan is invariably liked, for he will do a good turn for anyone if he can, and is always tactful and sympathetic. If Tolstoy has drawn a candid and unflattering picture of his own type of egoism in Konstantin Levin, he has drawn in Stepan a portrait of the other type of egoism—the amiable, Epicurean type—which is still more drastically complete.

Stepan's wife—Dolly, sister to Kitty Shcherbatsky—is a thoroughly natural and lovable creature; terribly disillusioned by her husband's infidelity, she is yet persuaded, for the children's sake, to forgive him and reunite the family; she bears with endless patience the worries his extravagance entails, and copes single-handed with the debts and the six children. It is hardly surprising if, at moments, she murmurs, and is almost inclined to think that the people who lead irregular lives (like Anna) have the best of it; it is only after a visit to Anna and Vronsky that she realises her own blessings, and understands that the tortures of a dissatisfied conscience are worse even than debts and a faithless husband. Dolly, however, stands by Anna in all her misfortunes; while women full of secret sins insult Anna in public, Dolly, the irreproachably virtuous, loves her to the end.

Aleksei Karénin—the husband of Anna—is brought before us in all his reality. We see the ugliness which so exasperates Anna—the ears that stick out straight, the habit of cracking the finger-joints—and we realise his cold vanity. And yet it is impossible not to be sorry for Karénin; he suffers a veritable martyrdom; that which he dreads worse than death—ridicule—overwhelms him at all points; he is crushed by the undeserved contempt of his fellows. Tolstoy shows us how little Anna's persecution was dictated by morality, for the cruelty accorded to the guiltless husband is just as great.

For a moment, when Karénin pardons Anna and Vronsky, he rises to real heroism, but it is a height to which he cannot keep; the poor man really is, as Anna well knew, a pretentious mediocrity; he is found out as a husband, found out as an official, found out even as a martyr; for a brief space, after the scene of the pardon, the reader is inclined to feel as if Karénin had been all along misjudged, but he returns to his usual self. When Anna has left him he falls under the influence of the stupidly sentimental Lidia Ivanovna; he becomes a convert to the most foolish form of spiritualism, submits Anna's fate to the decision of a medium, and refuses her a divorce because the medium pronounces against it—a course of procedure so extravagantly silly that it amazes even Stepan.

There are in the book many amusing and caustic portraits. One group—Lidia Ivanovna, Betsky Tverskáia, the Princess Miagkaïa, and Veslovsky—might have come from the pen of some eighteenth-century satirist; they have a Sheridan-like keenness and lightness of touch.

Lidia Ivanovna, especially, is excellent: she is a sentimentalist of the rankest type; having disgusted her own husband within a fortnight of marriage, she has ever since been incessantly conceiving romantic affections for one distinguished person after another; most of them are completely unconscious of her adoration, others ignore it, and the remainder are supremely bored; in poor deserted Karénin she finds at last a responsive object for her sentimentality and brings about, indirectly, Anna's tragedy.

CHAPTER VI

"MY CONFESSION"—"MY RELIGION"—"WHAT IS ART?" ETC.

We have seen that, in his fiftieth year, a great mental and moral change came over Tolstoy. The first of his religious works, *My Confession*, tells the story of this conversion, and it is a wonderful document—as intimate and candid as the confessions of Rousseau, but expressing a nature more profoundly moral, of deepest interest to us, moreover, as rendering a mood of doubt and despair so frequent in the nineteenth century that most of the century's leading minds have experienced something like it at one period or another.

It shows all the agony of a great soul, struggling in the deepest abysses of doubt, astray in a universe where all seems chaotic, dark, and meaningless, with no firm footing anywhere.

Tolstoy traces his own scepticism to the general scepticism of his age; with his usual incisive completeness he depicts for us, in one single paragraph, the whole mentality of such an epoch.

"I remember once in my twelfth year, a boy, now long since dead, Vladimir M———, a pupil in the gymnasium, spent a Sunday with us and brought us the news of the last discovery in the gymnasium—namely, that there was no God, and that all we were taught on the subject was a mere invention (this was in the year 1838).

"I remember well how interested my elder brothers were in this news; I was admitted to their deliberations, and we all eagerly accepted the theory as something particularly attractive and possibly quite true. I remember also that when my elder brother, Dmitri, then at the university, with the impulsiveness natural to his character, gave himself up to a passionate faith, began to attend the Church services regularly, to fast, and to lead a pure and moral life, we all of us, and some older than ourselves, never ceased to hold him up to ridicule, and for some incomprehensible reason, gave him the nickname of Noah."

Tolstoy goes on to analyse the situation as he saw it in his youth—that the men of his class did not obey in the least the precepts of the religion which they professed, but, on the contrary, lived in direct opposition to them; their faith had become purely conventional, having no influence upon their lives. He declares: "The open profession of the Orthodox doctrines is mostly found among persons of dull intellects, of stern character, who think much of their own importance. Intelligence, honesty, frankness, a good heart, and moral conduct are oftener met with among those who are disbelievers."

From the age of fifteen years onwards Tolstoy read many philosophical works; being in consequence far more self-conscious than his comrades, he was well aware of the disappearance of his faith; he ceased to pray, to attend the services of the Church, or to fast. He still possessed ideals of moral excellence, and honestly desired to make himself a good and virtuous man, but his passions were very strong, and he found himself almost alone in his search for virtue.

"Every time I tried to express the longings of my heart for a truly virtuous life I was met with contempt and derisive laughter, but directly I gave way to the lowest of my passions I was praised and encouraged."

Then follow the most bitter self-reproaches, describing how he yielded to all the sins and vices of his class.

It is curious and noticeable that Tolstoy does not perceive, in his first literary ambitions, any of the promptings of a higher ideal, but analyses his literary pretensions with contemptuous irony. He declares that he began to write out of vanity, love of gain, and pride. Here, again, he is surely too severe, for the most cursory reader of Tolstoy cannot but perceive that there is always in his work something true and genuine: sympathy with the lives of others, the pure and healthy joy of the artist.

Tolstoy continues with the same ruthless severity; it is doubtful if there ever has been a literary man more contemptuous in tone to himself and his fellows.

"The view of life taken by these, my fellow-writers, was that life is a development, and the principal part in that development is played by ourselves—the thinkers; the chief influence is again due to ourselves—the poets. Our vocation is to teach mankind. In order to avoid answering the very natural question, 'What do I know, and what can I teach?' the theory in question is made to contain the formula that such is not required to be known, but that the thinker and the poet teach unconsciously."

For a time, he says, he gladly believed this theory, because he earned a great deal of money and praise and everything else he desired. He firmly believed in the theory of progress, and that he himself, though unconsciously, helped it. After some two years, however, he became discontented, and it was his fellow-writers who disenchanted him; they were more dissolute even than his former military associates, and full of vanity. His connection with them, he declares, only added another vice to his character—that of morbid and altogether unreasonable pride. "Hundreds of us wrote, printed, and taught, and all the while confuted and abused each other. Quite unconscious that we ourselves knew nothing, that to the simplest of all problems in life—what is right and what is wrong—we had no answer, we all went on talking together without one to listen, at times abetting and praising one another on condition that we were abetted and praised in turn, and again turning upon each other in wrath; in short we reproduced the scenes in a madhouse."

There is surely something of unfairness here, and we may suspect that it was the proud and defiant spirit of Tolstoy which made him resent the contradictions of his literary friends. But, as we have pointed out, it was always Tolstoy's fault to underrate the intellectual powers of others, and also, to the end of his life, he underrated the value of intelligence in human affairs.

It was this pride which prevented him from nobly loving, as he might have done, men of the stamp of Turgénief, and, great artist as he was, it prevented him from that entire, humble absorption in his work which has saved the soul of many a lesser man. Tolstoy had to save his soul by a longer and a darker road.

On his tour abroad he still sought for satisfying moral ideas, and still found them, as he believed, in the conception of progress; he thought, at the time, that it had a real meaning.

"In reality I was only repeating the answer of a man carried away in a boat by the waves and the wind, who to the one important question for him, 'Where are we to steer?' should answer, saying 'We are being carried away somewhere.'"

Tolstoy refers to the execution in Paris as shaking his belief in progress, and giving him a real moral shock. The death of his brother marked another crisis in his mentality. The terrible sense of loss, the cruel fear of death in his brother, were things that made the doctrine of "progress" seem idle and tiresome.

Tolstoy next reviews his educational activity, and judges that too most harshly; he did not, he says, really know what to teach the children, so he evaded the difficulty by trying to make them teach themselves, with results which he describes as whimsical.

Shortly after this he married, and was so engrossed by his happy family life that he wholly ceased to inquire into the real meaning of life. He continued to write. "In my writing I taught what for me was the only truth—that the object of life should be our own happiness and that of our family."

After some ten years, however, he became hopelessly puzzled by the questions "Why?" and "What after?" and his torment increased until, by degrees, he could think of nothing else. His life had come, as it were, to a sudden stop. He could carry on the mechanical business of existence, he could breathe, eat, drink, and sleep, but he felt as if there were no real use in life, as if its meaning and its savour were gone. What was still stranger and more terrifying was that he could see nothing left even to desire.

"Had a fairy appeared and offered me all I desired I should not have known what to say.... The truth lay in this, that life had no meaning for me."

His life seemed to him to be a foolish and wicked joke played upon him by he knew not whom, and he refrained from carrying a gun because he was so continually tempted to suicide.

His mind dwelt on the inevitable miseries of human life; illness and death would most certainly come both to himself and to those who loved him best, and there would remain nothing of them but stench and worms.

He found his favourite reading at this time in Schopenhauer and Ecclesiastes. Solomon, the wisest man who had ever lived, declared that all was vanity, and he exactly agreed with him. There was no escape; the theory of "progress" did not apply at all to the individual life; philosophy was uncertain; science was marvellous in its methods and its intellectual power, but it led to no real result.

His conclusion was the conclusion of Schopenhauer and Solomon—that life was an evil poisoned through and through by the thought of death.

He began to study other men and their methods of escape. He saw that the young escaped this evil very largely through ignorance, by simply not perceiving the absurdity of Life, but it was impossible for him to take this means, as people cannot unknow what they know.

The second method was the Epicurean one; this was the favourite method with men of his class, because they really had plenty of means for enjoyment, and sheer selfishness prevented them from seeing or caring that the vast majority of men had no such resource. For this Tolstoy was too clear-sighted. The third means of escape was suicide, which was possible only to the strong and resolute. "The number of those in my own class who thus act continually increases, and those who do this are generally in the prime of life, with their physical strength matured and unweakened."

He considered this means of escape the worthiest, but had not the courage to make use of it.

The one thing that gave him pause was to see that the mass of men did not agree with this view and never had agreed with it; they continued to live as if life were a good thing and one that had meaning.

He turned his attention once more to the labouring classes whom he had always loved, and perceived that they held the true solution. He could not class them among those who failed to understand it, for they put it before themselves with quite extraordinary clearness; still less were they among the Epicureans, for their lives were rough, hard, and laborious; neither did they seek the solution in self-murder, for they looked upon that as the greatest of evils. Where, then, lay their secret? He answered: "In their religion." The peasantry were not like the upper classes; their religion was not for them a convention, but they really lived according to its teachings.

"Their whole lives were passed in heavy labour and unrepining content ... they accepted illness and sorrow in the quiet and firm conviction that all was for the best ... thousands and millions had so understood the meaning of life that they were able both to live and to die."

Tolstoy sought, passionately and despairingly, to gain this faith; he conformed to all the ceremonial requirements of the Greek Church, prayed morning and evening, fasted and prepared for the Communion; he took a pleasure in sacrificing his bodily comfort by kneeling, by rising to attend early service; he took a pleasure also in mortifying his intellectual pride by forcing himself to believe doctrines which he had formerly condemned.

At the same time his invincible intellectual honesty remained with him and tortured him. Thus when he took the Communion, he tried hard to persuade himself that it meant only a cleansing from sin and a complete acceptance of Christ's teaching.

"But when I drew near to the altar, and the priest called upon me to repeat that I believed that what I was about to swallow was the real body and blood, I felt a sharp pain at the heart; it was no unconsidered word, it was the hard demand of one who could never have known what faith was ... knowing what awaited me I could never go again."

The same invincible intellectual honesty made Tolstoy search into the whole teaching of the Church; he saw that its faith was irrational and merely a tradition, not the staff of life.

He found the Orthodox Church more and more opposed to what he believed: it conducted persecutions, sanctioned massacres, and blessed war. He was obliged to break with it. Once more and with humility he turned to the Gospels themselves; he drew from them what seemed to him the real essence of the Christian religion; from them and from the life of the common man—the Russian muzhik—he made up his own creed and lived as has been described.

Tolstoy followed *My Confession* with several other works. *The Four Gospels Harmonised and Translated* appeared in 1881-2. In this work Tolstoy extracts what he considers essential in the Gospel narratives.

My Religion appeared in 1884. It explains still further and in more detail Tolstoy's religious views. He bases his theories almost entirely on the "Sermon on the Mount"; he accepts quite literally the command against violence, which is henceforth the basis of his creed. "The passage which for me was the key to the whole was verses 38 and 39 of the fifth chapter of Matthew: 'It hath been said, An eye for an eye and a tooth for a tooth: but I say unto you, that ye resist not evil.' I suddenly for the first time understood the last verse in its direct and simple meaning. I understood that Christ meant precisely what he said.

"These words, 'Do not resist evil,' understood in their direct sense, were for me indeed the key that opened everything to me, and I marvelled how I could have so perverted the clear, definite words."

It is in this spirit that Tolstoy objects so profoundly to the whole organisation of modern society, since it is all based upon force. "Everything which surrounded me, my family's peace and their safety and my own, my property, everything was based on the law which Christ rejected, on the law, 'A tooth for a tooth.'"

From this precept of non-resistance Tolstoy deduces the wickedness of all war, however waged and for whatever object.

From the precept, "Judge not, that ye be not judged," he similarly deduces the wickedness and evil of all law-courts. From the precept, "Swear not at all," he deduces the evil of all oaths, and has no difficulty in showing that nearly all the things he thinks contrary to the law of Christ, "murder in wars, incarcerations, capital punishments, tortures of men," are committed only by the device of the oath, which substitutes a collective responsibility for an individual one, and so takes away from each man the sense he would otherwise have of committing an individual crime. There is in this book a very severe criticism of the Greek Church, which Tolstoy accuses of bolstering up and supporting all the worst evils of the time.

The Kingdom of God is Within You, 1893, is another long work which contrasts life on Christian principles with life as it is actually lived according to the maxims of the Church and State. There is an ironic and bitter analysis of the absurdities of Greek Orthodoxy, and an equally ironic and bitter analysis of the absurd conditions of modern Europe, which keep whole nations armed under the pretence that their ever-increasing military burdens are a way to peace.

With this group of works also we should class *What is Art?* 1899. It is the book which carries Tolstoy's asceticism to its climax.

There are many people who, though they sympathise with Tolstoy's ideals, decline to take seriously on the ground that he is a fanatic, and, if the matter be inquired into, it will usually be found that they base the accusation mainly upon his treatment of science and art.

Tolstoy has never a good word for science; he insists upon considering it as if it were concerned solely with abstract questions, and had no practical bearing upon the lives of men. The modern reader is overwhelmed with surprise by such an unwarranted assumption. Even if it were true that science is only valuable on its utilitarian side, we are still driven to confess that that utilitarian value is enormous; it has irrigated deserts, fertilised soils, improved animals, banished many diseases; it has made, even in the one occupation Tolstoy really reverences—agriculture—man's labour tenfold or a hundredfold more productive than it ever was before. If science has not yet effected the transformation of human life that it might have done, that is surely because our imperfect organisation of society prevents us from reaping the full value of its great and beneficent achievement.

And the case is even more astonishing when we turn to art. Tolstoy, himself one of the world's greatest writers, condemns almost all great art, from the Greek tragedians to Shakespeare, and almost all modern art—including, characteristically enough, himself. We must remember this truth, that Tolstoy was born an aristocrat, and that the members of aristocracies are nearly always cold to intellectual attainments; they belong to a privileged class which despises work and repudiates intellect. Tolstoy learnt, with all the energy of his strong soul, to exalt and reverence the once-despised labour of the common man, but he never learnt to esteem justly the intellect; he resembles Lord Byron, who, although a great poet, only condescended to the trade of letters, and regarded it always with a certain scorn.

Tolstoy is never, with his whole heart, a man of letters, and he is still less a scholar, for though at times he reads voraciously, it is almost wholly without system; there are the strangest gaps in his knowledge, and he is singularly impervious to all ideas except those with which he happens to be at the moment in tune.

However, *What is Art?* contains some admirable things. Tolstoy defines art as a human activity, the aim of which is to communicate to some other person the feelings which the artist has himself experienced. Art is effective in proportion as the artist's feeling is sincere and profound, and the expression of it clear; art is good or bad in accordance with the nature of the feeling transmitted; if the feeling is good it is good art, if the feeling is bad it is bad or debased art.

This is a fine definition, and well worth studying. From Aristotle downwards great critics have agreed that one aim of art is certainly "infection," and that the greater the art the more powerful the "infection" is likely to be.

Tolstoy asserts again that art is one of the great unifying forces of mankind, that it binds together different nations and different generations of men, and that that art is the greatest which has the most universal appeal. Here again there is little with which to quarrel. Tolstoy's definition of great art is almost St. Beuve's definition of a classic.

The amazement lies in the extraordinary manner in which Tolstoy has applied his own most excellent ideas. He loves Homer, and declares that his poems are truly national art, but he declines to admire the Greek tragedians. Why? They are surely as national as Homer himself. Again, he declares that the truly great artist ought always to express the best religious and ethical ideas of his time. Quite probably! Yet he denies this greatness to Dante, but if there ever was a poet who embodied the noblest religious thought of his epoch it was surely Dante! And Tolstoy condemns Goethe, who embodied the new religious conceptions arising upon the ruins of the materialistic eighteenth century. The fact of the matter is that Tolstoy does not really know the content of the world's great classics, and those whom he happens to praise—Homer and Molière—he appreciates, not because they are finer moralists than the rest (they are not), but because some accident has directed towards them his attention. It is curious to compare this essay with Shelley's *Defence of Poetry*; the underlying ideas in both treatises are identical; Shelley also says that the main aim of art is a unifying aim, and that the artist ought always, as a moral duty, to communicate the best impression that he knows. But what a world of difference in the catholic appreciation of Shelley! Shelley, also a great lover of mankind, never made the mistake of underrating the human intellect.

What is Art? had a sequel, to the English mind still more extraordinary, in two essays on Shakespeare published separately. In them Tolstoy condemns all Shakespeare, but singles out *King Lear* especially, mainly on the ground that the plot is absurd and the whole division of the kingdom fantastic. It is strange Tolstoy cannot see that *King Lear* is in essence, the thing he himself most admires—a moving and beautiful folk-tale; the very absurdity of the plot Shakespeare took over directly from the old story, and probably left untouched because it was so deeply embedded in his hearers' hearts.

Of course, it is not difficult to see why Tolstoy so dislikes Shakespeare—mainly because he throws such a glamour over aristocracy, and makes his aristocrats so noble in their sorrows, so radiant, generous, and joyful in their prosperity. Tolstoy is always insisting that aristocrats are not really like that—that they are selfish, stupid, and bored to death; but Shakespeare in glorifying aristocracy is only acting as the people, even in folk-tale and fairy-tale, have always done; they prove by that, it is true, nothing but their own naïve and inexhaustible goodness of heart. The truth is that, in belabouring Shakespeare, Tolstoy is doing the thing that would of all others, had he known its true import, have shocked him most: he is Tolstoy—the aristocrat—cuffing Shakespeare—the peasant's son—for being so like a peasant.

Tolstoy has often been blamed for making his uneducated Russian peasants the supreme arbiters of taste, but they would not agree with him about Shakespeare. A friend of mine, a Russian lady, told me she once saw *King Lear* played in a barn, with the roughest of accessories, before a peasant audience, and, at the conclusion of the drama, there was not a dry eye among the audience.

Still Tolstoy's eccentricities need not blind us to those ideas which really are stimulating and valuable. There is his warning against commercialised art—art is not a commercial product, and can never be "ordered" and "paid for" in the same way; there is the warning that schools of art can teach nothing but technique, and that, by an over-elaborate technique, talent itself is often crushed and spoiled; there is the emphatic statement that all great art should be catholic, and that the art which can appeal only to a limited coterie is, almost of necessity, poor art; there is the statement that all art should be as clear as the artist himself can make it, and that "contortions, obscurities, and difficulties" are mostly due to the vain attempt to hide shallowness; and finally, and most important of all, there is the statement that really great art can only be produced by those to whom life is a lovely, a joyous, and a noble thing.

CHAPTER VII

"THE POWER OF DARKNESS"—"THE KREUTZER SONATA"—"RESURRECTION"

Tolstoy has written but few dramas; among these stands pre-eminent the tragedy entitled *The Power of Darkness*. The scene is laid among peasants, and the work is didactic; as is the case with *Resurrection*, its aim is to show the possibility of redemption even for the most fallen.

The drama opens with an exceedingly effective situation: Anisya, the second wife of an invalid husband, is in love with the vigorous and powerful young labourer Nikíta, and reproaches him jealously because his father wishes him to marry.

Matrónya, Nikíta's mother, is a wonderful study in the evil side of maternity—its colossal egoism and its willingness to sacrifice everything to the welfare of a beloved child. Matrónya condones her son's adultery, because she hopes that it may lead, when the invalid husband is dead, to a good establishment.

The old father—Akím—represents the good genius of the piece: Nikíta has got an innocent girl into trouble and his father wishes him to atone by marrying her; he insists that moral welfare is the only real welfare, and that, in comparison with it, nothing else matters, and the whole terrible course of the play shows how right he is. Akím represents in the drama the one element of real moral beauty, the one light in the "inspissated gloom," and it is characteristic of Tolstoy that he should ascribe this position to the man upon whom society has thrust its filthiest and most repulsive task; Akím, able to find no other honest work, has become a cleaner of cesspools, and has grown so repulsive outwardly that his own wife feels sick when she approaches him. Nor is he a man of intelligence; his habit of continuously repeating his words makes him appear almost half-witted, and his wife terms him "an old mumbler."

The Power of Darkness produces a terrible effect on the nerves, for the gloom is as dreadful as in *Macbeth*, and it is not relieved by heroic battle or the splendours of a crown; it is to the last degree sordid—the concentrated essence of sin. Yet the chain of moral causation is linked as firmly as in *Macbeth*, and we are shown, in the same unflinching way, how crime haunts and sears the conscience, and how the worst punishment of sin is that it leads on to ever more and more sin.

The conflict between the evil genius and the good genius—Matrónya and Akím—turns first on the girl whom Akím has seduced, and Matrónya wins, persuading her son to repudiate the unfortunate orphan whom he has so deeply wronged. Also, to hurry matters on, she persuades Anisya to give her husband sleeping-powders which are really poisons.

The second act shows us the working out of this crime: with tragic irony we are made to see that Anisya has no particular objection to poisoning her husband; what she does mind is that he dies so slowly; his horrible sufferings wring her heart, yet she hates him the more for the grief he causes her.

Anisya could not maintain her cruelty were she not continually urged on by Matrónya; she has not even the consolation of Nikíta's support, for Matrónya will not permit him to be told; again with grim tragic irony she declares that he is so kind-hearted that he could not kill a chicken.

In the third act events have moved a stage further. Nikíta and Anisya are married, but further than ever from happiness! Nikíta has learnt of the crime; he regards his wife as a murderess, feels her hateful and repulsive, and, with his usual soft-hearted sensuousness, has turned for consolation to his wife's half-witted stepdaughter—Akoulina. Anisya has to bear all alone the dreadful consciousness of her guilt; she has the bitterness of seeing Nikíta spend on another the money for which she, as she feels, sold her soul; Nikíta beats her, and her passion for him enslaves her so that she can make no real protest. She is surprised herself at her own weakness: "I haven't a grain of courage before him. I go about like a drowned hen."

Anisya's only hope is to get rid of Akoulina by marriage, but the neighbours suspect something and hold aloof. Even Matrónya, always on her son's side, has turned against the unhappy daughter-in-law; the one person who pities her is old Akím, who warns his son that he is acting against God and on the road to ruin.

Again Tolstoy reminds us of *Macbeth*; his peasant heroine has gained all she desired, but it is hollow and worthless, and she envies her victim in his very grave.

In the fourth act we have the punishment of Nikíta. Akoulina is to be married, for the sake of her dowry only, but her confinement comes just before the wedding should take place, and, if the child's existence is once known, it will ruin all. Nikíta, as usual, wants to throw the burden on his wife, but Anisya refuses absolutely.

Matrónya, callous as ever, urges her son to the murder of his infant; with tragic irony in her speech she declares that it is such a little thing, it can hardly be counted as human at all. Anisya too urges him on, not with callousness but with a more terrible hate.

"Let him also be a murderer! Then he'll know how it feels.... I'll make him strangle his dirty brat! I've worried myself to death all alone with Peter's bones weighing on my soul. Let him feel it too."

Nikíta, always weak, gives way, and commits the murder, but it sickens him to the very soul.

In the fifth act we see the long-delayed punishment of Matrónya. To the end she remains callous; she cannot understand the moral sufferings of Anisya and her son, but she can be reached through her son's worldly ruin, and that is what occurs.

Nikíta cannot endure the hideous consciousness of his guilt. "When I eat, it's there! When I drink, it's there! When I sleep, it's there! I am so sick of it, so sick! ... Even drink takes no hold on me."

He ponders suicide, but reflects that this would only be a new crime, and at length he nerves himself, before all the wedding guests, his old father helping and assisting him, to make full confession.

There is no splendour in this drama, not even the splendour of crime, but Tolstoy has good warrant in depicting evil as he does; he shows the worst feature of evil as being its insufferable meanness and dirtiness, and the same truth is driven home by *The Kreutzer Sonata* and *Resurrection*. But though this drama is so gloomy it is not despairing; the one point of light glows and kindles till it overpowers the whole; even in the heart of the darkness God has made manifest His power.

The Kreutzer Sonata probably ranks with *Anna Karénina* as being the best-known of Tolstoy's productions. It had in England and elsewhere what might be termed a *succès de scandale*. The emphasis laid upon it is, in some ways, unfortunate; it serves many people as an introduction to Tolstoy; they read it, are repelled, and explore no further. The truth is that it stands almost alone among Tolstoy's works; the same elements are present, the same ideas are discussed elsewhere, but they are nowhere else brought to a focus of such intensity and concentrated in such powerful expression.

The piece is almost pure Strindberg; it represents that woman-hatred, that loathing of marriage, that helpless rage against physical passion, of which the Swedish author has made himself the chief European exponent. The situation is exactly the sort of situation Strindberg delights in: husband and wife bound together by a purely sensual passion which they both abominate but cannot, either of them, control; the paroxysms of indulgence followed by paroxysms of mutual loathing; the endless quarrels; the reciprocal jealousy; the miserable and shallow infidelity; and, as a climax, the miserable, vanity-inspired murder. But, though the subject is almost pure Strindberg, Tolstoy is infinitely more just to women than Strindberg could contrive to be.

For Tolstoy's wretched and morbid hero, roused to insight by his own cruel deed, can place the blame where it rightfully belongs; he can see that the real fault does not lie in woman as woman, but in woman as man has corrupted her. With an incisive truth that Strindberg cannot rival he gets to the very root of the mischief and reveals it in man's own sensuality. He makes a serious and passionate plea for purity in men; he speaks with horror of the doctors who encourage vice and of the pseudo-science which declares it necessary. The moral corruption which ensues does not begin and end, as people falsely think, with women of loose life; on the contrary, it pervades the whole of society. The man who has "fallen" takes a wrong attitude towards all women; he regards them, even the pure and innocent, as being created for his physical pleasure. Tolstoy, like Meredith, finds in the demand for "innocence" and "bloom" mainly the desire of the voluptuary to whet his own jaded appetite. The result is the degradation of women; they are all, even to most innocent young girls, turned into sexual lures, made to expose their arms and bosoms in immodest ways, and to provoke the appetites of men.

The hero goes on to analyse the miseries of his unhappy marriage; here again they are traced to the root-cause—the excessive sensuality of the husband, who degrades his wife and destroys her health and her nerves, thus exciting in her incessant irritability, which, in its turn, exasperates and annoys him.

The only remedy, Tolstoy insists, is to treat woman as a human being, to give her full human rights, and not consider her simply as a possession. At present woman is treated as an object of pleasure, and becomes a degraded and demoralised serf. In her turn she enslaves man by demanding endless luxuries which his labour must produce.

Once the exposition is complete the story advances with Tolstoy's usual masterly skill. The psychology of hate has never been drawn with a more fearful accuracy. To the end the hero is self-rigorous; he acknowledges that he killed his wife, not because she violated his love (he had none), but simply because he regarded her as a property in which he had an inalienable right. He feels, and makes us feel, that this is the most horrible feature in the whole repulsive tale.

Resurrection, the last of Tolstoy's great novels, was written after he had, as he thought, definitely resigned fiction. Wishing to help the Doukhobors, he took up and completed the unfinished manuscript of this book, which shows that his hand had in no way lost its cunning. Less purely a work of art because far more didactic than *War and Peace* or *Anna Karénina*, it is in every way worthy of the author of both. It tells a single story of the most wonderful and moving pathos. We are introduced to the hero—Prince Dmitri Nekhlúdof—at the moment when he is summoned to take his place on a jury. The first case is one of murder; three people are accused, among them a prostitute named Máslova, and in her Nekhlúdof recognises to his horror a certain Katusha whom he had first known as a pure and innocent girl, and whom he himself had seduced. He tries to stifle his conscience; he assures himself that "everybody" does these things, and that he is not to blame for Máslova's fate; but, notwithstanding his struggles, the conviction is borne in upon him that he is morally responsible both for the woman's hideous degradation and for her presence in the dock.

With the most consummate art Tolstoy introduces us first to the foetid and wretched atmosphere of the law-court, with the story of the poisoned merchant, and the horrible description of his half-putrefying dead body, and then, by force of Nekhlúdof's recollections, shows us the magical contrast of Katusha's pure and innocent girlhood.

There is no love story in literature rendered with a more poignant charm. Katusha is the one woman whom Nekhlúdof had really and truly and poetically loved; he loved her when he was himself innocent, and his love had the aroma of Paradise, never, in all his later life, to be recalled again.

Katusha was a poor girl, the daughter of a gipsy tramp, whom his aunts had educated, half as a servant and half as a companion. She is very beautiful, refined in her manners, exquisitely tender; he loves her with a love full of reserves and mysteries, incredibly sweet, transfiguring the whole world. Nekhlúdof goes away; he returns, but, in the meantime, he has tasted of vice, and he is no longer the same. When he sees Katusha again the old innocent poetic charm revives once more, but it has now to contend with what Tolstoy called "the dreadful, animal man." For a moment the better nature conquers. No scene in all Tolstoy's pages is more lovely than that of the Easter Mass, when Nekhlúdof rides to the church early in the morning across the snow, sees it brilliantly lighted, the priests in their gorgeous vestments, hears the glorious Easter hymns, and feels as if all the joy, the tenderness, and the beauty were for Katusha and for her alone.

"For her the gold glittered round the icons; for her all these candles in candelabra and candlesticks were alight; for her were sung these joyful hymns.... All ... all that was good in the world was for her."

But Nekhlúdof has been corrupted by his own evil life; he cannot for long control his passions, and, in spite of the poor girl's piteous fear, he takes advantage of the fascination he possesses over her to ruin her.

It is a night of spring, with a white mist above the melting snow, the ice tinkling and breaking in the river. Nekhlúdof twice summons Katusha, and twice she evades him, but in the end it is done. Never has the charm and romance of passion been more wonderfully rendered, but Tolstoy makes us feel this seduction terrible as a murder.

And the worst detail of all, the one that Nekhlúdof remembers with burning cheeks, is that, when he left, he paid Katusha by thrusting into the pocket of her apron a hundred-rouble note.

The trial proceeds. Máslova, though manifestly innocent, is condemned by a technical error and sentenced to Siberia. Nekhlúdof determines to appeal, and, moved by his remorse, he decides also to make himself known to her and ask her forgiveness.

In the meanwhile we are introduced to the household of the Korchágins, whose daughter Nekhlúdof is expected to marry. We see the contrast between the wretched lives of the prisoners, who suffer and have always suffered from every form of privation, and the debasing luxury of the Korchágins, which produces, not happiness but only ennui and fatigue. We see the contrast between the conventionality and tiresomeness of Nekhlúdof's relations with the young princess and the pure poetry of those earlier relations with Katusha. The *mariage de convenance* is evident in all its weariness.

These scenes are closely linked with the main purpose of the book: what Tolstoy wishes is to make his reader feel that the whole penal system is wrong and false, partly because the people who come under it are mainly the victims of a cruel form of society, and partly because those who condemn them are, in their own way of life, no better but probably far worse. The Korchágins have to their credit a long series of evil deeds, floggings and judicial murders, gluttony and sexual offences.

Nekhlúdof sees that, compared with these people, Máslova and the rest are almost innocent, and grows more and more disgusted with the life of his set. He makes himself known to Máslova.

Tolstoy has no sentimentality, and he cannot pretend that the horrible life which his heroine has led has not made any essential difference; on the contrary, it is her profound moral corruption which is, as Nekhlúdof at once realises, the most hideous consequence of his sin. When she first recognises his interest, she has no special feelings towards him, but only wishes to make use of him in order to extract from him money for drink. But, when he asks her forgiveness, she overwhelms him with foul abuse. She cannot believe in his real penitence, but thinks that, just as he once used her for his physical pleasure, so now he wishes to make use of her to save what she calls his "dirty soul."

Tolstoy now tells us the story of the seduction as it appeared to her, and adds details of a terrible and haunting pathos. The poor deserted girl realised that she was about to become a mother; she was aware that the train in which her lover travelled would pass through the station at a certain hour, and determined to make an appeal to him, but she lost her way in the darkness and arrived too late. She was not able to speak though she saw him through the lighted carriage window; in the night and storm, and darkness, injuring his child which she bore, she rushed along by the train as far as she could go, and saw it carry him away faster and faster. In that hour something vital—belief in God and in man—snapped in Katusha. Unable to free herself, she sank lower and lower into vice, until she arrived where Nekhlúdof found her.

When he implores her forgiveness she is roused to fury because he tortures her by reminding her of her lost innocence, and forces her to realise all the abominable degradation she has endured. Nekhlúdof is, however, true to his repentance; he insists that he is willing to marry her if she will consent, but, if not, he will follow her to Siberia, and do all in his power to alleviate her lot.

As soon as she realises that this is being done genuinely, for her and not for "other-worldliness," she is touched and moved.

From this point onwards she begins to return to her true self—not her former self (Tolstoy's art is far too subtle for that), but a self deepened and saddened by suffering. This gradual awakening is wonderfully depicted; the daring title which Tolstoy gives his book is truly merited; indeed the revival of a dead body seems almost a small thing as compared with this amazing transformation of a human soul. Never since the Magdalen has the story of a fallen woman been treated with such a noble beauty.

We are accustomed to sentimentalising over the courtesan who at last conceives a "pure" love, but Tolstoy does not write in the spirit of a Dumas or a Victor Hugo. Máslova is sick of passion; she and Nekhlúdof redeem each other, but, in the ordinary sense, they do not love. Máslova throughout the book is one of the most real women in fiction; we see every detail of her appearance—the white skin, the black curls over her forehead, the eyes black as sloes and slightly squinting, the expression of willingness with which she turns to anyone who addresses her. It is strange how Tolstoy insists on that detail of the "slightly squinting" eyes; it haunts us as it must have haunted Nekhlúdof. And her mind and heart are as real as her bodily personality. Tolstoy, as we have seen, always did possess a marvellous power of maintaining a consistent personality while permitting his characters to change and develop, but nowhere else has he shown it in a manner quite so magical. From the pure romantic young girl to the prostitute, from the prostitute to the woman redeemed and sweetened and saved—his heroine is still herself throughout.

It is in the hero that Tolstoy's talent for once fails him, since Nekhlúdof is too obviously only a mouthpiece for Tolstoy's own reflections.

We could understand him if the change in him were essentially a spiritual one similar to that in Máslova, but what Tolstoy has portrayed is rather a profound intellectual dissatisfaction, so deep and so far-reaching that it could only have been experienced by a man of the greatest intellectual and moral power, a man of genius, while there is nothing in Nekhlúdof's previous life to suggest that he was in any way out of the ordinary.

He is too slight to undergo the tremendous mental experiences of a Tolstoy, and we cannot believe that he does; nevertheless, the experiences remain, and tremendous they are. *Resurrection* is an indictment of the whole of society as we know it now, and it is impossible to read it without the gravest searchings of the heart. It is true that some of the most serious counts in the indictment apply mainly to Russia. More than with the West, Russian society is divided into two great classes—the rich who have everything and are idle, and the poor, who have nothing and labour; in England we have—in the professional classes and the better artisans—numbers who possess a very fair share of the amenities of life and also do valuable work.

Again, it is impossible to say of any large class in our prisons, what Tolstoy says of the Russian political prisoners: that they get there because they are the best members of the community, more intelligent, more unselfish, and more courageous than their fellows.

Still, when all allowances are made, the greater part of Tolstoy's indictment lies good against the whole of modern society: in all countries there are classes ruined by idleness, leading lives which, as Tolstoy says, are "a mania of selfishness," consuming in senseless luxury the toil of thousands. Everywhere there are other classes, degraded by poverty and misery, who spend their whole lives in labour, and reap for themselves hardly any of the benefits of their toil. Everywhere men permit many thousands of people to become criminals simply because they are helpless and defective, and then, when they have made them criminals, debase and torture them further by imprisonment. Tolstoy is convinced from the bottom of his heart that the whole penal system is cruel, savage, and unjust, and it is almost impossible to read him without feeling the same.

He is certain that the majority of men are naturally good, and that the so-called "wicked" are either the victims of our social system, or else of a physical and mental weakness they cannot control.

It is easy to object to the "sordid realism" of *Resurrection*, and to declaim against its morbidness and misery, but this morbidness and misery are not Tolstoy's fault; they are inherent in the social system which we, all of us, uphold and, in wishing to escape from them, we are trying to escape from the consequences of our own acts and principles.

To use one of Tolstoy's own phrases, he "rubs our noses" into the mess we have made of civilisation; he makes us realise the horrors in which our depths abound—the vice, the dirt, the foul obscenity, the vermin—and people who think that great literature exists merely to amuse and soothe object with furious vehemence.

The great heart of the writer is stung with anger and pity and shame that men—our brothers—should be so debased and tortured. He is goaded to madness by this outrage on our common humanity, this insult to God.

Tolstoy is a realist because he has the courage to face facts as they are, because he believes that the cause of true morality is never served by evasions and concealment, because this concealment is, in itself, one of the chief allies of vice.

Though a realist Tolstoy is not, in essence, a pessimist. There is more real pessimism in one chapter of Thackeray than in the whole of *Resurrection*, for Thackeray thinks men despicable, and despairs of their being otherwise.

Tolstoy, like Rousseau before him, is convinced that human beings are naturally good, and that, if human nature becomes base, it is only because it has slipped from the divine ideal, the spark of God, which exists in each one of us. Like his Master, Tolstoy is assured of the redeeming power of penitence and tenderness.

Our redemption may come to us from within, through the struggles of our own soul, or by the aid of another, but it is always accompanied by sweetness and compassion; loving-kindness is the true centre of our being; the supreme sin—the sin against the Holy Spirit—is to transgress, no matter for what motive, the law of love in our dealings with our fellows.

Our so-called "principles" and "ideals" do not excuse us; any ideal, whether patriotism or justice or honour or religion, becomes reprehensible when it makes man act inhumanly to man; the supreme test, always and invariably, is the test of brotherhood.

CHAPTER VIII

THE INFLUENCE OF TOLSTOY

Tolstoy's influence is a great and growing one, both in Europe as a whole and in England. He is the most powerful and impressive critic of our existing social order.

We have seen that, in certain respects, Tolstoy stands apart from the humanism of Europe; it is impossible to read him without seeing that he is imperfectly acquainted with the achievements of the human mind, and very imperfectly indeed with their value. He emphasizes the fact that he is not a humanist by his intense dislike of the Renaissance and his continual references to it as a period of moral decay.

But his very limitations are, in some respects, his strength. He has no unreasonable reverence for civilisation which, to use one of his own favourite words, can "hypnotise" him into accepting civilisation's defects.

He insists on trying it, fairly and squarely, by its conformity to the needs of man, and in condemning it when it does not conform to man's noblest ideal—brotherhood.

And Tolstoy is the latest and the greatest of the mystics; the essence of his creed is the Christian mysticism of the Middle Ages, stripped of its ecclesiasticism and supernaturalism, but insisting most strenuously on the old ideal of the Catholic Church—the brotherhood of all men through religion. According to Tolstoy's creed the Spirit of God exists in each one of us, the highest good for man is to cherish this Divine Spirit within himself, and the supreme duty, both for the individual and for the social order, is to further the true Christian unity.

Moreover, Tolstoy's rule of life is the old monastic rule of poverty, chastity, and labour, though he substitutes for obedience to an "Order," the harder and more rigorous command of immediate obedience to a man's conscience.

The vital spirit of mediæval religion, its unquestioning, wonderful, literal acceptance of the commands of Christ, lives still among the Russian peasants; what Tolstoy has done is to take this spirit, shake it free from ceremonies and dogma, rescue the true and glowing fire from its incumbent mountains of ashes, and insist, with all the vehemence of his most vehement soul, that it is the true light of the world.

Our Christianity, he tells us, is sick to death; it has become so entangled with paganism and rationalism that it is hardly worth while calling Christianity at all; indeed we find in some modern writers—Nietzsche and others—the frankest paganism, calling Christianity a "slave-morality," and declaring it unworthy of the free. Tolstoy declares that Christianity is not founded on rationalism but is divinely inspired; he is original only so far as he insists that this divine inspiration occurs not in any Church or tradition, but in a man's own heart; like the seventeenth-century Puritans, he accepts the Bible as his guide, but he rejects the Old Testament and relies entirely upon the New.

And Tolstoy's influence is so profound because he announces the dissatisfaction which, secret and overt, is assailing us on all sides; we are, none of us, really satisfied with our civilisation as it stands, we all desire a better one, and Tolstoy's is the most powerful and eloquent amid those voices which are summoning us to emerge from the dwelling which has grown too narrow and to build a new.

This is why Tolstoy, the preacher of non-resistance and peace, is really one of the most powerful of revolutionaries. And, paradoxical as it may sound, he is also one of the most powerful of individualists.

It might be imagined, at the first glance, that Tolstoy stands at the opposite pole from such a writer as Ibsen—Ibsen the uncompromising individualist, who preaches self-realisation at all costs, and breaks furiously through our so-called "duties," and Tolstoy who preaches self-abnegation, self-sacrifice, and humility.

But, when we look closer, we see that there is a unity underlying all seeming differences; both men are profoundly dissatisfied with the "ideals" of present-day Europe; they insist that all values must be revalued, that all the old "duties" must be questioned, and rejected if they will not stand the test of the new morality.

And who is to be the supreme arbiter? Both Tolstoy and Ibsen answer: "The man's own soul."

No one would trample on the old "duties" more thoroughly than Tolstoy; he insists that his countrymen must renounce all they have previously held most sacred, their "duty" to the Czar, their "duty" to the State, to their oaths, even in the last resort to their families; for, like Ibsen, he finds the "family snare" one of the worst and deadliest.

Both Ibsen and Tolstoy are quite agreed that, when a man is sure of himself, he should, if need be, stand alone against the world.

Tolstoy is, indeed, one of the strongest of individualists, and, as the terrified Greek Church saw when it excommunicated him, his doctrine of "peaceful anarchy" is the most tremendous solvent for society's hierarchy that has ever been conceived by the mind of man.

We may sum up briefly the leading channels in which the influence of Tolstoy runs.

He is one of the most powerful forces in favour of what may be termed "social justice." The conscience of civilised Europe is more and more declaring that some reconstruction of our social system has become imperative, and Tolstoy is among those who have done most to arouse this conscience. That he overstates in some ways, that he is too hard on the upper classes—all this is possible, but there is so much in his indictment which is true and accurate that we all feel guilty before him.

Again, he is one of the most powerful of all apostles of peace. He is aware, as we have seen, of the nobler side of war. He knows that it really can and does rouse an enervated aristocracy to something finer (in *War and Peace* he shows us the actual process); but he also realises that the vast majority of the people—the working class—are moralised and strengthened by their daily toil. For the mass of the people war is as needless as it is futile. Tolstoy shows that the ends for which it is waged are nearly always childish and absurd, and his unflinching realism has made him an unrivalled exponent of its horrors. Ruskin and Carlyle have both preached against the horrors of war, but Tolstoy is more effective than they because he knows it at first hand.

In the third place, Tolstoy is one of the most effective critics of our penal system and capital punishment. Here again there are many other writers—such as Mr. Galsworthy and Mr. Bernard Shaw—who follow in the same track; they also declare that the faults and sins of the rich, who almost escape our penal system, are no less serious than the sins of the poor, who fall victims to it; they also declare that our penal system is mainly torture and revenge, that it does not cure but only brutalises, and that the majority of its victims are not foes of society but only people who are too weak to keep straight, and whom our harsh industrial system flings to the wall. But here again, though Tolstoy agrees with other men in his diagnosis of the evil, his exposition of it is far more masterly than theirs. It is not possible to name any other work which shows the tragedy and terror of prison life in the same manner as *Resurrection*.

In social purity, again, Tolstoy's has been one of the most potent voices. Many people think that he carries his asceticism unnecessarily far, but, when we think of the corruption which has invaded so large a part of Europe, we can see that he heads a much-needed revulsion. And here again he excels by the extraordinary power and fidelity with which he shows the evil results of loose living: its tragic cruelty to the seduced woman, its power of corrupting, by a kind of reflex action, even those who would seem most remote from its sphere. And Tolstoy has not limited his condemnation to "irregularities"; he condemns the immoral marriage no less severely, and has given a most drastic analysis of the vices which underlie "respectability." Tolstoy will not allow virtue to consist in anything so cheap and easy as mere legality.

Again, his influence also tells in the direction of simplicity of life. Many people are arriving at the conclusion that modern civilised life is too complex, that it achieves not real refinement, but luxury which enervates and ostentation which vulgarises. Tolstoy joins the cult of the "simple life" by another road: by pointing out the immensity of the labour which luxury entails upon others.

And finally, we may point out that in art also the age is feeling its way towards an attempt to realise, consciously or unconsciously, the Tolstoyan ideals.

We are beginning to ask for the simplification of art, for its deliverance from over-elaborate technique; we are beginning to see that it cannot be truly deep and profound unless it is also national and of the people; that Tolstoy is essentially right when he declares that art, by cutting itself off from popular inspiration, becomes barren and sterile.

BIBLIOGRAPHY

BIOGRAPHIES OF TOLSTOY

Life of Tolstoy. Aylmer Maude.
Life of Tolstoy. Holland.
Life of Tolstoy. Birukoff.
Recollections of Tolstoy. Behrs.

ESSAYS AND STUDIES

Tolstoy and his Problems. Aylmer Maude.
Tolstoy as Man and Artist. Merejkovski.
How Tolstoy Lives and Works. Sergyenko.
Ideals and Realities in Russian Literature. Kropotkin.
Leo N. Tolstoy. A. Löwenfeld.
Essays in Criticism (2nd Series). Matthew Arnold.
(French) *Tolstoi et les Doukhobors, faits historiques réunis par* J. Bienstock.
(German) *Graf Leo Tolstoi*. Anna Seuron.

TOLSTOY'S WORKS

(*Specially notable works are marked with an asterisk*)

1852. *Childhood.**
1853. *The Raid.*
1854. *Boyhood.**
1855. *Memoirs of a Billiard Marker.*
    The Wood Felling.
1856. *Sevastopol** (Complete).
    The Snow Storm. Two Hussars. A Landed Proprietor.
1857. *Youth.** *Lucerne.*
1858. *Albert.*
1859. *Three Deaths.** *Family Happiness.**
1863. *The Cossacks.** *Polikoushka.*
1869. *War and Peace** (Complete).
1872. *A Prisoner in the Caucasus.*
    God Sees the Truth.
1874. *On Popular Education.*

1877. *Anna Karénina** (Complete).
1878. *First Recollections.*
1879. *My Confession.**
1880. *Criticism of Dogmatic Theology.*
1881. *What Men Live By.*
     Church and State.
1882. *The Four Gospels Harmonised and Translated.*
     On the Census.
1884. *What I Believe.**
     The Decembrists.
1885. *Where Love Is God Is.**
     Two Old Men.*
1886. *What Must We Do?*
     Ivan the Fool.
     Death of Ivan Ilyitch.*
     How Much Land Does a Man Need?
     Eyas. The Three Hermits. The Candle.*
     The Power of Darkness.*
1887. *On Life* (Philosophical Essay).
1889. *Culture's Holiday.*
     Kreutzer Sonata.*
1891. *The Fruits of Culture* (A Comedy).
1892. *Articles on the Famine.*
1893. *The Kingdom of God Is Within You** (Against War and Government).
1894. *Season and Religion.*
1895. *Master and Man.**
1898. *What is Art?*
1899. *Resurrection.**
1900. *The Slavery of Our Times.*
     Thou Shalt Not Kill.
1905. *The One Thing Needful.*
1906. *Shakespeare and the Drama.*
1908. *I Cannot Be Silent.**
     Posthumous. *Father Sergius.**

www.ingramcontent.com/pod-product-compliance
Lightning Source LLC
Chambersburg PA
CBHW031410040426
42444CB00005B/503